The Show Starter™ Reality TV Made Simple System, Vol. 1

ભ – છ

Ten Steps to Creating and Pitching a Sellable Reality Show

by DMA/Donna Michelle Anderson

MOVIE IN A BOX BOOKS

With special thanks to: my family for championing me throughout the writing of this book and the producing career that inspired it; J.M. Morris for your enthusiastic seminar support and book notes; the network execs, show runners and staff members who mentored me, assisted me and believed in my systems; and the seminar attendees whose fire for joining the reality TV-selling ranks made this book a joy to write.

Published by MOVIE IN A BOX BOOKS

First Printing, December 2006

THE SHOW STARTER REALITY TV MADE SIMPLE SYSTEM, VOL. I

ISBN-13: 978-0-9787150-1-4
ISBN-10: 0-9787150-1-2

PRINTED IN THE UNITED STATES OF AMERICA

Movie in a Box Books can be purchased for personal, business and educational use or sales promotion. They are available at quantity discounts.

For information, please contact Movie in a Box, 14622 Ventura Blvd #333, Sherman Oaks, CA 91403 or visit www.movieinabox.com/books.

CONTENTS

INTRODUCTION
Who Needs to Read a Book to Sell a Show?

Who needs to read *The Show Starter Reality Show Made Simple System, Vol. 1*? The shorter question is: Who doesn't?

You do not need to read this book if: a) you already have sold a reality TV show *and* successfully stayed attached to it *and* it aired *and* it got good ratings; or b) you are on the BlackBerry speed dial buttons or MySpace friend lists of numerous broadcast and cable network executives.

Everyone else, if you have watched enough people compete to eat bat droppings, propose to strangers after one hot tub scene too many or have their less-than-perfect homes/faces/lives made over by telegenic gurus, and you believe that you, too, can sell a reality show, please...read on.

Since you have purchased or been given this book, I am fairly sure you agree with and, in fact, are motivated by, at least three of the four following statements:

1) You have an idea you think would make a great reality show;

2) You watch reality TV and not-so-secretly believe you could do as well or better coming up with show ideas;

3) You are not making the money you'd like to be making and are planning for a reality windfall by selling a show; or

4) You are more interested in selling a reality show
     than actually working on one. Unless it is your own.

Some of you are private clients of mine from my show
runner training sessions. I have met others of you at my
Show Starter™ reality TV seminars, including: "The
Realities of Reality TV," "From Concept to Network Deal: 10
Steps to Selling Your Own Reality Show" and "Reality 201:
10 Steps to Running a Streamlined Reality Show." Still
others are staff members from my shows who want to
replicate some of my systems for their own projects. And if
all of these interactions are any indication, for most of you
reading this book, your biggest motivating factor in trying to
sell a show is #3: the big bucks. So now would be a good
time for our first "reality check."

Listen and believe: selling reality shows is not a "get
rich quick" scheme. It is not even a "get rich slow" scheme.
There is no real money to be made in selling reality shows!
The money in reality TV comes from *producing* those shows.
Not one show, not two shows, but multiple 13-or-more
episode series. Yes, there are millionaires in reality TV, and
most have them have more than one show on the air, and
they own the company that physically produces those shows.
Reality is a volume industry.

You have just read my words, but, frankly, you do not
believe them. What about Mark Burnett? you ask. He was
a gazillionaire after *Survivor* broke out! Quite probably
true. In fact, Mark Burnett's extraordinary success has
made him the Pied Piper of reality TV. Everyone is skipping
down Hollywood Boulevard behind his legacy, assuming if
they sell one show, they, too, will rake in product placement
millions and enormous production fees. But the industry
has learned a lot since the early days of giving producers so
much for their shows. They no longer underestimate the
power and revenue stream of reality programming. So now
they keep it to themselves and share it with only a select
few. Okay, really just with Mark and Tyra Banks, members
of an elite club not currently accepting applications.

Is it possible that you might be the exception to the
current rules? That you, too, might develop and sell the
zeitgeist-defining juggernaut that earns you untold millions?

Well, sure, anything is possible. But as a good friend of mine likes to say, why are people always trying to make a career out of being the exception when there is plenty of success to be had just by being the rule?

I was on a reality producing panel recently alongside the financial guru/VP of a mega-reality production house here in Los Angeles. The attendees, only *one* of whom actually had worked in reality TV, would not stray from questions about how to sell their own shows. I stopped and asked why they were so intent on selling a show rather than working in the industry first and learning how it operates. The uniform response was "to get paid!"

That was my cue to write a dollar amount on a piece of paper and flip it upside-down on the table, hidden from my fellow panelists. I announced that I had written down the largest sum of money I believed they could possibly make from selling their first reality show. What did they think that was? They called out a range of figures: "$50,000!" "$25,000!" "$100,000!" I turned to my fellow panelist, the guru/VP, whom I had never met before that evening, and asked him for his figure. He said he probably would not pay them anything just for an idea. But at most, he would pay them "$5,000" all in, for their idea and their involvement in the show.

I turned over my slip of paper. The amount? "$5,000."

Why then, one attendee wanted to know, do you make reality TV?

You make reality TV because you want access to an international platform to reach real people and change their lives. You make it because you have very strong opinions on how people should dress, date, live, cook, decorate, work and behave. You make it because you are incredibly curious about human behavior and how it can be altered, improved or debased. You make it because it is an incredible challenge to develop a show, get it through production and make it to air, and you are a glutton for punishment and sleep-deprivation. You make it because it is both creative and logistical, hilarious and distressing, rewarding and confounding. If reality shows are "train wreck TV," then reality production is "train wreck living." You want to keep driving, but the disaster in front of you is too compelling to pass by.

When the moderator took over the questioning, we finally were able to discuss how to actually work in the reality industry. Because unless you own a production company that has more than one show on the air (so multiple fees can pay for business overhead and leave room for at least a small profit), the way to make money in reality TV is by working on shows and, ultimately, running them for other people, as I did. But that does not stop people from wanting to create, pitch and run their own series, as I did.

What *does* stop people from creating and pitching their own series is not knowing how the reality industry works. That is what this book is for. I am writing it as a guide through a very established process that you will be expected to know and follow as you try to sell your first show.

Before you begin, please let me state several seemingly contradictory facts about the process that lies ahead:

1)   The reality TV industry has a bottomless hunger and programming need for new shows; yet

2)   The reality TV industry makes it virtually impossible for you to pitch them new programming without personal, insider contacts or a top-level agent; and

3)   Even if you manage to do it, there is virtually no benefit to you in selling your first reality TV show; but

4)   I am excited to teach you how to do just that.

Show Starter, Vol. 1 is for anybody who is attempting their first sale of a reality TV show. Whether you currently work in reality TV or not, there is a simple and savvy system you want to learn before you toss your brilliant idea onto the craps table of broadcast and cable programming for the first time.

Even if you are shooting for a second or third sale, the Show Starter™ system will give you a streamlined approach to covering your bases and expanding your possibilities. Of course, four or more sales in, you could just use the book as a doorstop as you saunter into your network buddy's office and say, "Here's the show: it's [latest Hollywood hottie]... marrying a different guy every week... and the contestants compete to see who shoots the best honeymoon video. The winner gets 10% of the online bootleg profits." Sold.

It is my hope that you are reading this book as a roadmap, a soon-to-be dog-eared reference tool so you will feel more confident, informed and prepared for the challenge ahead. But I realize you may only be skimming it, looking for the shortcuts to reality riches. Yeah...about that... That chapter is not in here. Sorry. If even after what you have read so far, you are still counting on selling a reality show as a quick way to earn loads of money without doing any work, know this: the easiest part of this process is going to be reading this book. Everything after that is Hard Work.

This absolutely is not a book about how to make mountains of money in reality TV. This is a book about how to craft reality TV shows you can actually pitch and sell. Whether you actually sell a show depends on these wildly variable primary factors:

1) How compelling your idea is to the buyers you meet;
2) How well you execute that idea into a viable show format;
3) How desirable the talent is you attach to the show;
4) How the cost of your show measures up against the buyers' budget and potential return;
5) What the current trends are in the reality marketplace;
6) How relentless and inventive you are in your efforts; and, most importantly,
7) If you ever meet and pitch to a person who is both enthusiastic about your show and in the position to get it made.

Of course, I cannot guarantee you will sell a show even by following the Show Starter™ system to perfection, due to those same wildly variable primary factors (and more that only Hollywood can shock and awe you with). I *can* promise, however, that that this book will teach you how to effectively conquer those primary factors and that trying to sell a show will be infinitely less frustrating, discouraging, intimidating and angering if you learn and apply this system first.

Five simple requests before we move forward:

1) **Realize right now that disdain gets you nowhere in this industry.** If you believe that all reality shows are utter trash, you will win no points with the producers and executives who have sacrificed the past 10 years of their lives, both professionally and personally, to create this new, exploding genre of entertainment.

2) **Accept that if you have never worked in the reality TV industry, that by trying to sell a show, you are expecting to start at the absolute top of this field with no training or experience.** I equate this surprisingly common syndrome to being airlifted to the top of Mt. Everest. Sure, you are at the top, but you have no idea how to survive the climate or make it back down alive. Worse, no one respects you for being at the top if you were flown there; the kudos are reserved for people who survived the mountain climb. Those people also are the ones who stay at the top for a while, surrounded by all the helpful Sherpas they worked with during the ascent. And the real discoveries, fun and friends in this business come from that crazy climb anyway. Don't be an "Everest Boy"! (That's not gender-specific, by the way; women can be "Everest Boys," too.)

3) **Commit now to building and utilizing a "Reality Research Lab."** Identify at least three shows you like to watch that are similar in tone or format to the show you hope to sell. Go rent those shows, TiVo them, catch reruns, watch them on VOD. Just get at least a season's worth of at least three shows. I also recommend getting a DVR (digital video recorder), if you don't own one yet, to keep up-to-date on current shows so you can create knowledgeable, timely pitches. (Is that expensive? Yes. Will you be able to sell a show with no personal cash investment? No.)

4) **Forget about trying to make money without spending any!** Set aside real "seed money" so you can survive and thrive in this process. Throughout this book, we will build your development budget to

give you an idea of how much you might need to invest to effectively pursue this passion.

5) **Embrace that pitching actually serves two purposes.** First, it gives you a shot at selling a show, but that is only a 50/50 possibility over which you have no final say. The second function of pitching, over which you have far more control, is to open industry doors and keep them open for *future* pitches. In other words, you pitch to sell both your show and yourself. If either one leaves a positive lasting impression on a network or production company executive you meet, the pitch was a success.

So even if you do not sell a show at the end of developing a solid product and taking your first round of meetings, it is my hope that you will have established many new relationships that will put you positively on track to a sale.

Do I think you're crazy to try to do this? No. I *hope* you are. It is the only way to enjoy the bumpy ride ahead. As I mentioned earlier, over the past 10 years, I have set up, produced and run a wide range of reality TV shows and have pitched, sold and run my own. Now let me show you how it is done.

Chapter 1

Step #1:
I Have a Great Idea for a
New Reality Show!

Congratulations on your new show concept! Not everyone trusts their gut and creative muse enough to dream up an original idea. Now for the bad news. There is not a thing you can do with a concept.

Let us please start with this crucial shift in perspective: having an idea is not the *end* of the show-selling journey; it is actually the *beginning*. If you have what you feel is a terrific concept, the next step is not to set up pitch meetings with networks and producers (or to mail, fax or e-mail your idea unsolicited to their offices). It is to *develop* the idea.

Not only can you not sell an idea for a show, you cannot even legally protect it. That's right, you cannot copyright an idea. Or safeguard one by mailing it back to yourself (stop doing that! When you are ready, a copyright is only $45).

> To make it simple, **you cannot copyright or sell an idea** for a reality show. You can only copyright and sell the original and detailed description of how you will *execute* that idea as a show.

Please let me explain why I am so passionate about an interesting idea not being enough to pitch or sell a show. As I speak nationwide on "The Realities of Reality TV," the number one question I get is how audience members can take their one-sentence show concept and exchange it for a network check. Hear me out on this. Selling your "idea" to a network to make a show would be like you sketching a picture of an office tower then asking Big Downtown Corporation (BDC) to hand over a $40 million check so you can start building their new suburban headquarters. Uh...slow down.

Before they pay you to create the vision in your picture, BDC first would like to see your architectural degree, license and certification. And what other buildings you have built. They want to talk to previous employers, contractors and vendors who have worked with you in the industry. They also want to see your detailed blueprints and contingency plans for each phase of the project. Maybe you could even present a series of 3-D models to them? And by the way, what is your schedule for building the corporate headquarters, and how soon can they get a glimpse of your budget for the project?

That is when you tell them...and this is awesome...that you actually are *not* an architect...and you have never even built a building before. In fact, you have no idea if this building is even structurally possible or how that would be achieved. But you are addicted to skyscrapers! You dreamed of being Mr. Brady when you grew up (even if you were a girl)! Plus, you've spent a lot of time downtown staring up at the buildings, and no one has ever drawn a skyscraper sketch that looked just like this. This is your very own, original concept! Now where is your money?

You understand why BDC is not about to hand you or any other sketch artist millions of dollars to create something based on a picture when you have no experience or training to construct a habitable building. Even if it is a gorgeous concept, BDC's money is going to go to whatever company actually fully *designs and builds* the building—and the person who can effectively oversee that process.

So now you understand why broadcast and cable networks (the "nets") won't hand you millions, not even thousands, of dollars to create something based on an idea when you have no experience or training to create a shootable show or only have work experience that is not yet at that level. That is why I am writing this book. The Show Starter™ system fills in the blanks between your idea and your final pitch so you can create something that actually can be sold. It is not incredibly hard. It is just not as easy as many expect it to be.

Wait a minute, you say! I don't want to learn how to make reality TV shows! I don't want to work on anyone else's anymore either! I just want to sell my clever idea and make my money and get on with my life. Wait a minute, I say! You have mistaken reality TV for those other lucrative, union-negotiated, minimum-fee-establishing, created-by-credit-giving, residual-paying arenas of Hollywood (like fiction TV). Sorry. Again, as hard as it is to sell a reality show; it is even harder to make money off of one! As I said before, in reality TV, the money is not in selling the shows; it is in producing them.

One final reason I want you to stretch far beyond just having an idea for a show: the less you actually bring into a pitch meeting, the less chance you have of remaining attached in any way to the show if it eventually sells. This industry has its own special business model, which this book will help you navigate more successfully so you can craft a detailed reality pitch package that you will have grounds to stay an active part of.

If you still long to just make some one-shot cash that will translate into future passive income, may I recommend you put down this book and read my *1-3-5 Story Structure Made Simple System* book instead? You will still have to work hard (my own expertise came from my early years as a story analyst at a major Hollywood film company), but the *1-3-5* book will teach you how to write a structurally sound screenplay, and navigate that sales process.

However, if you still want to sell a reality TV show because you actually want to *make* one...let's go.

Chapter 2

Reality 101

Just to make sure we are discussing the same thing, here is a quick breakdown of what reality TV is, relative to other types of television programming. (If you already work in reality TV, you might want to skip this chapter. Nah, just go ahead and read it; it will be an important refresher course!)

TV programming generally is broken down into two realms: "scripted," or fiction television, and "unscripted," or non-fiction television. Non-fiction is a broad category that defines virtually everything you watch except for sitcoms, hour-long dramas, television movies and soap operas. So news programs, game shows, documentary shows, talk shows, etc., all are considered non-fiction programming.

The "baby" of the non-fiction family is reality TV. Its birthday is widely stated as 2000, with CBS' launch of *Survivor*. Actually, that show, and the many similar shows that followed, launched and popularized the second of two reality genres, commonly called the "competitive" or "elimination" genre. But from many people's point of view, nearly 10 years before *Survivor* became a reality rock star, what we now know as reality TV was born with the runaway hit MTV series *The Real World* in 1992. That show, and its multiple spin-offs and imitators, created the first and other reality genre, known as the "vérité" or "slice of life" genre.

So there are two types of reality TV, "competitive" and "vérité." Within those two genres, or "formats," are endless categories of programming, from Lifestyle programming (makeovers, fashion, cooking, decorating) to Travel to Health & Fitness to Procedural (criminal, medical) and more. An example of a "competitive," "fashion-based," "lifestyle" show would be Bravo's *Project Runway*, while a "vérité," "fashion-based," "lifestyle" show would be TLC's *What Not to Wear*. Or a "competitive health" show would be NBC's *The Biggest Loser,* while a "vérité health" show would be *Intervention* on A&E.

One common mistake people make is confusing reality TV, especially the vérité format, with documentaries (like PBS' groundbreaking *An American Family*). Both film real people in real settings. Documentaries, though, require impartial observation, recording what takes place and editing it into a narrative presentation. Reality TV, on the other hand, is not a passive or observational experience! In reality TV, we create and control the environment and/or activities our subjects engage in then record what they do as a result.

> To make it simple, reality TV drops **real people into controlled experiences** and crafts compelling story from the participants' reactions.

Competitive reality shows are, of course, highly controlled environments, ensuring the ability to create conflict and advance story in every episode. But vérité reality shows rely on controlled environments, too. Examples of fully controlled vérité worlds would be the plastic surgery immersion that is *Extreme Makeover* or any other makeover show. More loosely controlled vérité environments include the fishbowl campus experience that is BET's *College Hill* or many of the character-driven shows, like A&E's *Dog the Bounty Hunter*. But even such so-called "docudramas" have a guiding hand, usually due either to removing participants from their familiar environments and dropping them into a controlled residential or working world (like the aspiring chefs in *Hell's Kitchen*), or dropping controllable talent into other people's worlds (like *The Simple Life*).

The only thing we do not control in reality TV is how our carefully cast participants *react* to the world we expose them to. These shows are not fake! The best ones are just exceedingly well cast to maximize conflict, humor and, ultimately, story. Reality casting is all about creating a compelling, distinct and even incendiary "mix" of subjects, whether they all are participating together as a group, as on NBC's *The Apprentice*, or there is a different main participant each episode, as on MTV's *Pimp My Ride*. I always say that casting a reality show is like the college admissions process. You are not really looking for preconceived stereotypes ("the princess," "the bitch," "the snob," etc.), as many people believe. You are looking for a group of people whose diverse experiences complement, conflict with and challenge each other, so everyone will change during the show.

Many industry insiders, including me, believe passionately that reality TV is made in the casting phase. In fact, shows often are picked up on a "casting contingent" basis, meaning that if the production company cannot come up with the right mix of participants to assure compelling TV, the show will not be produced. As you develop your show, remember it is the magic of excellent casting, mixed with good storytelling and some luck, that makes or breaks the reality shows you love...and love to hate.

Once you grasp the truly vast scope of reality TV, it is harder to hear—or to say—"I hate reality TV!" There is just too wide a range of shows to trash in a single judgment. Yes, there are dominant trends, with the first five years of the millennium evolving from cutthroat competition shows (like *Big Brother*) to titillating dating and romance shows (like *The Bachelor*) to feel-good, community service-based shows (like *Extreme Makeover: Home Edition*). Do you have any personal preferences?

Take a moment now to list at least three reality shows you have watched and enjoyed (if you don't have three, stop trying to sell a show and do some more front-end research. Watch more shows!). Now write down whether they have competitive or vérité formats. Next, figure out what category each falls under: Lifestyle, Health & Fitness, Travel, Sports & Gaming, Procedural, Relationships & Romance, a hybrid of several categories, etc. Finally, pay close attention to how controlled the experience is for participants in the show.

Feel free to make your Research Lab notes right here in the book; that is why we chose spiral binding!

SHOW #1: _____

Format:

Category:

Control-Level:

SHOW #2: _____

Format:

Category:

Control-Level:

SHOW #3: _____

Format:

Category:

Control-Level:

Get a sense of your own taste, and you will have an immediate compass for developing shows you yourself would love to see.

Chapter **3**

Who are the Real Reality Players?

As you prepare to try to sell your first show, let me next equip you with a straightforward look at who the players are on the sales floor. Again, for reality TV veterans, you may want to move on to the next chapter, but stay and refresh yourself on our industry's detailed money trail.

To make it simple, the three key players in the reality TV industry are the **advertisers** that pay for shows, the **networks** that air the shows and the **production companies** that make the shows.

The Advertisers

Like all other areas of TV, the people who pay for the shows are at the top of the heap. And that is not the networks; it is primarily the advertisers.

Every year, advertisers gather at a glutton-fest of network previews called the "upfronts" in New York. There, the various networks unveil massive dog-and-gilded-pony shows with their biggest stars, live performances and, most importantly, new programming schedules, to convince advertisers to give them mega-ad dollars for the coming season. That's right, advertisers often buy into series before they are even shot or broadcast. Or, at least, they *did*.

The nets took a beating at the 2006 upfronts, with advertisers withholding substantial dollars from network ad sales departments. Some blame it on the ad industry wanting to spend more on "new media" (broadband and mobile content, etc.) or for targeted brand integration inside of shows. All the nets know is they did *not* get their expected springtime ad dollars for their new shows later in the year. Which meant the nets had to come out of pocket more to pay for programming to fill their schedules.

So where did all of that ad money go that the nets didn't get? Here is where it did not go: to a place you have access to so you can sell a show. We will get back to ad dollars later in the book. Just know that when the nets get less outside money, they take an even closer look at cheaper programming. Hello, reality TV!

The Networks
The networks are right below the advertisers on the money ladder since they buy shows and, more importantly, distribute them to the public by airing them. In fact, until the recent new media explosion, cable and broadcast nets completely controlled your ability to bring a show to an audience. And for the most part, they still do, if you are not yet an indie TV producer with your own infrastructure for casting, shooting, posting and delivering product directly to an online or mobile audience you can effectively harness.

Not to worry, new media will be addressed in a follow-up Show Starter™ series. But it is yet another business model to develop new media formats, monetize them and market them to an audience, and it certainly is a bigger pile of seed money! So for this book, we will surge ahead with the most common way still to finance a project, which is to sell your show to a network, get that show produced, and have the network air it.

The Production Companies
Right underneath the networks in the hierarchy are the production companies who actually make TV shows. And

here is the one area where reality TV rules and the rest of the industry can only watch in wonder. In reality TV, independent production companies still produce the vast majority of the shows we see. Until the new media boom, in fact, non-fiction TV was the last frontier in the entertainment industry that mighty corporate conglomerate America did not completely control.

In scripted television like sitcoms, as soon as the networks could legally own their own programming, they wiped out virtually all of the independent production companies by producing their own content (and eliminating outsider profits from already lethally expensive shows). But non-fiction television, and reality TV, is far less expensive to make. And the explosion of new cable networks and tiers has created a massive demand for programming that the nets cannot possibly meet—or feel they do not need to if they can find someone else to do it on the cheap. Which they can.

Many networks actually do have in-house production companies that produce reality programming for their own channel, other networks and syndication. But those shows make up a small percentage of the hundreds of shows out there, most of which are being cranked out by indie production houses. So in reality TV, the production companies are king. They are the ones who actually execute an idea into a hit show. They are the ones pitching new content to the networks, partnering with newcomers to produce their content, or getting calls from net execs to produce new shows the networks have dreamed up. *Reality TV happens at the production company level.*

Production companies are run by one or more "executive producers" who own the company. Those same executive producers may or may not be the people who oversee the actual shows. **The producer who actually oversees a given reality TV show is called a "show runner."** Depending on how the production company structures production, a show runner might be an executive producer, a co-executive producer or a supervising producer. That is why the industry uses the umbrella term "show runner" to identify the person or people responsible for overseeing all elements of production and liaising with the network on a reality TV show.

Unless a show is being run by the actual owners of the company, which is common only at smaller houses, the show runner and most of the staff on a show are actually freelance hires. That means staff members, from production assistants to show runners, often work on several shows at multiple production companies in the course of a year. The downside of this freelance universe is that employment is not guaranteed (though jobs are fairly plentiful), and only a few companies offer benefits. The upside is that working at multiple companies expands your contacts dramatically, which can be a huge plus when you start pitching your own show.

Now that we know who the players are and how they play their game, it is easier to understand the cash flow cycle in reality TV. Advertisers give money to the networks. Networks dispense some of that money to production companies to produce shows. Production companies use most of that money, keeping a small percentage as a fee, to produce shows that the networks then air, along with the advertisers' commercials. (Additional ad dollars sometimes flow in to networks or shows thanks to brand integration, which I will discuss in more detail later on.)

Advertisers make their money from purchases by consumers who watch the show. Since the networks own the shows they air, they continue to make money from advertisers and consumers by redistributing shows via affiliate channels and syndication, new media outlets, DVD sales and more. And while few production companies have any ownership in their shows, they might get to "participate" in any of those additional network profits if their contracts allow for this (which is a coup in reality TV!).

You

What I want you to grasp from this chapter is who has the money to buy your show (advertisers and networks), who can distribute your show to a television audience (networks), who can actually produce your television show so it can air (production companies), and how they all make money from the deal. Do you see where you fit into this smooth operation as an independent, freewheeling, idea-creator? That's right. Nowhere.

If you just have an idea, you need to convince either a network to buy it or a production company to bring it to a network to buy it, which I will explain in great detail later in this book. For now, believe this: network development teams and production companies are drowning in a sea of independent, freewheeling ideas, both their own and the dozens they are pitched every single week by people like you. So in their eyes, you and your idea bring nothing to the table.

But if you bring a fully executed show format (the steak) with an irresistible element attached (the sizzle), with a legal contract binding you to the sale in some *organic* way (the knife), well, now, they are going to be much more excited to see you. And they will ask you to sit down and stay a while, if only because they cannot legally get rid of you. So let's talk about transforming your show idea into a far more substantive reality TV format that you can sell and be a part of (okay, and maybe even realize a little money from).

"REALITY CHECK"

Throughout this book, you will find a series of pledges that summarize what you have learned so far–and what you must commit to do in order to craft and pitch a sellable show. Here is the first one.

 Pledge #1: I will read and apply the entire Show Starter™ system, without skipping any chapters, steps or exercises, before I attempt to sell my first show.

Chapter 4

Steps #2 and #3: Crafting Your Pitch and One-Sheet

Now that you have a number of original ideas, you are ready to create the three documents that will help you execute, pitch and ultimately sell your show:

1) a one- or two-sentence sell called a "**pitch**";
2) a one- or two-page summary called a "**one-sheet**"; and
3) a five-page or longer detailed show execution plan called a "**treatment**."

No skipping this chapter, reality vets! This is the heart of the system. It is not only about learning the terms but about breaking these documents down into their most essential elements.

> To make it simple, you will execute your idea in three development stages: a **pitch**, a **one-sheet** and a **treatment**.

The first thing I want you to do to begin developing your idea into a real show format is...let it go. Speak it aloud, pat yourself on the back for your unusual genius, then begin a creative process that may or may not yield a show that has anything to do with this initial idea.

The second thing I want you to do, and this will send shudders through the collective spine of all my former staff members, is *database* your ideas. For reasons you will understand when we advance to the sales process, having one idea for a reality show will pretty much get you nowhere. You are going to need many ideas to sell even one. So right now, please, open a new spreadsheet, create a new word-processing table, get all sexy with a new relational database program (like Access or Filemaker Pro), just somehow begin a list of your ideas and what type of shows they are. Here is an example of a starter Pitch Database (see if you can spot the real pitch on the list):

Date	Name	Description	Genre	Category
053104	The Dirty Truth	Workaholic dads compete in a laundromat to see who can make their whites the whitest.	Competitive	Lifestyle
090604	Club Darwin	Professional gamblers face off against a team of trained monkeys on the casino floor to prove if gambling is, indeed, about skill or just dumb, furry luck.	Competitive	Sports & Gaming
080205	Keeping Up with the Joneses	A team of charity workers help different families with the surname Jones raise funds for research for loved ones with rare illnesses.	Vérité	Health

Which one is the real pitch? Here is a little history to set it up. When my agent first sent me out to sell shows, I had built a database of over one hundred pitches, and I could not wait to meet network executives and wow them. Still, one net exec would not meet with me, telling my agent, "She's not going to pitch me anything I haven't heard before." I sent my pitch list to my agent and told him he could guarantee the exec at least one completely original pitch. And when I arrived at the network, I opened with *Club Darwin*! The network executive laughed, asked some logistical questions about executing such a crazy show (which I answered in detail), and he later announced a funnier title would be *Champs & Chimps*. Then he leaned forward and listened to the rest of my pitches with interest.

I did not sell a show that day, but I did build a relationship with an exec who now knew I respected his time–and understood his network's brand. (Other initial pitch meetings have yielded more amazing results, including show runner job offers.) I am going to return to *Club Darwin* throughout the book to demonstrate how to develop even the most outrageous concept into a sellable show.

Now add at least one of your ideas to your database. (In case you are not in front of a computer, just draw a table that looks like this–but with more space to write):

Date	Name	Description	Genre	Category

See how committing your idea to the page frees you from the anxiety of forgetting it? Great. Be sure to transfer any written notes to your computer so you can build a database you can easily search and track during the pitching process. And don't forget to regularly back your database up, and print and file it, as it grows. That eases anxiety, too.

Congratulations! You now have at least one idea before you, broken down into its most basic components for the industry: genre and category. You might even have learned a bit about your own taste in reality TV. Now take a moment to work the idea a bit. What would your competitive show look like as a vérité experience? Could your Sports & Gaming idea also translate into a Health & Fitness show? Don't skip past this brainstorming phase! This builds your database and makes you more versatile in "the room" when you try to sell a show by training your creative muscles to adapt your show on the spot to a network's particular brand.

Let's give this a try with *Club Darwin*. Right now, it's 12:38 pm on Planet DMA. Below is a database with my original *Club Darwin* pitch, and I am going to brainstorm two new versions of the show in a different genre and category:

Date	Name	Description	Genre	Category
090604	Club Darwin	Professional gamblers face off against a team of trained monkeys on the casino floor to prove if gambling is, indeed, about skill or just dumb, furry luck.	Competitive	Sports & Gaming
090106	Darwin Days	Whiny slackers are paired up with chimps that live their lives for one day. From driving golf carts to staffing the register at the mall jewelry shop, we find out if the chimps can show these chumps that their lives aren't so bad.	Vérité	Lifestyle
090106	Monkey's Uncle	A quirky monkey trainer and his ape sidekick take on a family's bratty kids to see if banana chip treats, monkey bar breaks and peanut shell fights can help bring peace to a house that's turned into a zoo.	Vérité	Relationships & Romance

Okay, it's 12:45 pm, and I now have three ideas. And I was working with monkeys vs. humans as a premise! I now have two more shows in my database (and who doesn't love *Darwin Days*)?

I am challenging you right now to come up with two new and different shows based on your original idea. So add two more rows (like below) to your table and fill them in.

Date	Name	Description	Genre	Category

Stop! Are you skipping past the grid, hoping to just read for now? Please take a moment to do the few simple exercises I present in the book before moving on. It is important to get used to doing creative work on demand to work in this industry–or even survive a pitch meeting–and you will need the results from above to do the next step in this book. Give it a shot. Come up with two new ideas.

Great! Now that you have three ideas to work with, it is possible your original idea may not even be your favorite version of the show. That is the power of letting your idea go. Now pull out a file folder, name it with your show title, and print out your Pitch Database (unless you already wrote it on paper). You have just begun your official "Show File"! That file will hold all of the research, legal documents and other paperwork you generate as you develop this concept. Your Show File needs to be "grab-and-go" if you get a last-minute call or meeting. It only has one piece of paper in it right now...but not for long.

From here, you need to expand at least one of your three ideas into the written documents you need to shop the show: a pitch, a one-sheet and a treatment. Again, your first step in developing your show is a simple "pitch," which is usually only a few sentences long and is the short-and-sweet sell of what your show is about. Second, you need a "one-sheet," a one- to two-page summary of the basic premise and sizzle of your show. Third, you need a "treatment" for the show, which is a five-page or longer, fully detailed breakdown of how the show will be executed.

In this chapter, we are going to review the core components of a pitch and of a one-sheet. The treatment comes later because we are still one major element short of a sellable show for first-timers! So first pick your favorite idea of the three, and let's begin.

The Pitch

Yes, it can be confusing, but the word "pitch" in this industry is a verb meaning to present a project to potential buyers, and a noun that means both the brief presentation of your project *and* the meeting where that presentation takes place. To keep things simple, which is how I like them, I am going to use another term for your one- to two-sentence pitch. It also is sometimes called a "logline."

What is a logline? Let's start with what a logline, or a reality show, is *not*. It is not a general statement about where a show takes place or who is on it. I cannot list all of the baffling chats I have had with people who say "I have a great idea for a show" and then say something quite generic like, "It takes place in a ski resort." Or "It's models and wrestlers dating." No, no, no. You have just blown your shot at getting the ear of someone inside the industry who knows buyers for shows that actually *are* great.

If anyone, including me, has ever stopped you in the middle of a pitch and said, "I don't get it," or "Nothing really happens," here is the key to reality TV. Reality TV shows generally change people's lives. Thanks to a new room, a battle for a job, a borrowed wife, etc., whoever participates will not be the same person at the end of the experience as they are in the beginning. Even if a central talent is the heart of a reality show, it is because they themselves live a life that guarantees conflict and change every episode.

> To make it simple, your **pitch** or **logline** must immediately establish the mission of your show, who is on that mission, and how that mission will change their lives.

Your logline is an immediate indicator of your credibility as a show creator. If you do not present the most basic, industry-expected elements of a good logline, an exec cannot conceive that you know how to put together a sellable show. Plus, their time is valuable, and you have just showed them you did not think it even was worth learning how to discuss a show correctly. Therefore, they will not listen to anything else you have to say. As those of you who have attended my industry panels know, execs really do feel this way!

Your logline also is the strongest indicator of the sellability of your show itself. Why? Because the harder it is to narrow down the intent, execution and appeal of your show to a few sentences, the clearer it is that your idea has not yet taken full form. So you must learn how to concisely present the information that actually matters to a buyer when you get even a 30-second shot at a pitch. Here are a few examples of loglines for hit shows—watch how clean and simple the descriptions are, then we will break down the Five Key Elements of a great pitch:

- A mix of people from the modern world are abandoned on a desert island and forced to compete in "tribes" for food, tools and luxuries, with one person ruthlessly voted off every episode. The last one standing is the "survivor."

- Five wickedly witty gay men with diverse lifestyle expertise play Professor Higgins to a hapless straight male's Eliza to make him and his house over for an important event.
- A team of home improvement do-gooders has only one week to construct an entirely new house that will help a deserving family facing an overwhelming personal challenge live a better life.

I cannot imagine you need me to tell you the names of these shows (if so, e-mail showstarter@tidalwavetv.com—and use an alias). A clean logline is that distinctive, and an original show is that original.

Now let's use those loglines to dissect the critical components of even the most basic pitch:

1) The "**Who**": It is important to establish who exactly will be on your show. That includes any talent or hosts as well as any participants. Keep your "who" as narrow as possible! That leaves room for spin-offs and sequels. Don't say "people" or "guys" or "kids." Say "spoiled kids" or "marriage-minded women." It will help buyers immediately understand the energy of the show and the values of the people who will be on it.

2) The "**What**": This is a simple statement of what relatable madness the subjects and hosts are going to engage in each episode, or over the course of the series.

3) The "**Conflict**": This is missing from virtually every pitch people run past me. Remember that reality TV is still story-telling, and story is based on conflict. The easiest conflicts you can create and *control* are between:

   a. your subjects and a new environment (*Survivor, Wife Swap*);

   b. your talent and the show's subjects (*Queer Eye, Super Nanny*); or

   c. your talent/subjects and external forces, like limited time or resources (*Extreme Makeover:*

Home Edition's one-week clock or *Sensible Chic's* design-cloning challenge on a fraction of the high-end budget of an original inspiration room).

Another great by-product of conflict is comedy, or humor. Unless you want to cast stand-up comics on every show, if your show is not too dark in mission, structure a world that guarantees "the funny," like the misguided wannabes auditioning for *American Idol*.

4)   The "**Change**": American audiences relate most to stories that cause people and their lives to change. Internal change is the most powerful (think of life swaps like *Trading Spouses* and *Black. White.*); external change is the most visual (think of any makeover show or, well, *Black. White.*). Make it a point to include both in your show. And be sure to make the change organic to the participant's experience on the show. (It would make no sense to give people makeovers while living alone on an island or to give families a million bucks for switching kids for a week.) The Change also establishes the stakes of the show. What are your participants risking (privacy, comfort, pride) to win something (money, a husband, sobriety, etc.)? On *Wife Swap*, for example, women are willing to stake their entire identities and self-worth as wives and moms for the chance to help another family and maybe learn how to make their own families better. On many other shows, the stakes are simpler: participants sacrifice something for a big fat cash prize.

5)   The "**Eye Grab**": This is big. Since this is television, sell what the audience will *see* that will glue them to the screen. Do they need to see a giant scale with fat celebrity has-beens huddled in the balance? Well, yeah, just ask any *Celebrity Fit Club* fan. Ask yourself this: what visuals do *you* describe to your friends when you talk about

your favorite reality shows? You will equally memorable and *unique* visuals in your own.

Take a moment to re-read the sample loglines and make sure you can identify the Who, the What, the Conflict, the Change and the Eye Grab in each of those shows. Pretty easy, right? Now let's give it a try with *Club Darwin*, based only on this pitch:

'Professional gamblers face off against a team of pea soup-flinging monkeys on a casino floor to prove if gambling is, indeed, about skill or just dumb, furry luck. The team that collects the most chips wins a grand prize."

1) The **Who**: Our cast includes professional gamblers and trained monkeys.

2) The **What**: The humans and monkeys are competing against each other in gambling events (slot machines, roulette, blackjack, etc.).

3) The **Conflict**: Professional gamblers will fight to the death not to be beaten by monkeys. Monkeys will want to destroy the casino and play with, rather than against, the gamblers. Neither has much control over the risk, luck and fate that defines gambling—but the humans believe they do.

4) The **Change**: At the end of the show, either the humans will have to accept that dumb luck can outperform their intellect and skill...or they will be one big fat cash prize richer. The monkeys will not change, but they might find out they enjoy pulling slots and flinging soup.

5) The **Eye Grab**: Um, monkeys...are gambling... against uptight humans...in a casino...and flinging pea soup.

Now give it a try with your own show! Write or type out the following list and complete it for one of your three pitches:

THE FIVE KEY PITCH ELEMENTS

SHOW NAME _____

1)   The **Who**:

2)   The **What**:   .

3)   The **Conflict**:

4)   The **Change**:

5)   The **Eye Grab**:

Ready to turn it into a logline? Not yet! File your work so far. At this point, your Show File should have two items:

<u>SHOW FILE</u>
- Pitch Database
- Five Key Pitch Elements

Now it is time to delve into your Reality Research Lab from the opening chapter (*page 6*).

Watch the first episode of each of the three shows in your Lab. It had better be crystal clear exactly *who* will be involved, *what* they will be required to do, what internal and external *conflicts* they face, what potential internal and external *change* they will make for what *stakes* and what *visuals* really grab you in the show. If these elements are not clear, stock new shows in your Lab!

Now for the next Lab exercise. You know these shows well; you probably watched them every week when they aired. Can you easily reduce them to their essence? Better yet, when you describe one of the shows to others, can they identify it, or do they feel you have missed the very reason they watch it?

Try now to write clean loglines for your three Lab shows, with the Five Key Pitch Elements (feel free to write in the book):

Logline–Show #1:

Logline–Show #2:

Logline–Show #3:

Great. Now is it finally time to write your own logline? Actually, still not yet. A logline is a summary, a condensation or crystallization, of the core mission and strengths of your show. And you do not have a show yet. We need to develop the idea further, then at the end, we will reduce it back down to logline gold.

The One-Sheet

My favorite part of developing a show is working out the one-sheet, which is less challenging than writing an entire treatment or nutshelling that into a brief, effective logline. A one-sheet is the high-energy, entertaining and/or gripping reduction of your show's essential components (the Five Key Pitch Elements expanded, attached talent, etc.). It is the written equivalent of what you will say in a pitch meeting if your simple logline makes an exec lean forward and say, "Tell me more."

To make it simple, a **one-sheet** is the one- to two-page summary of what your show is about. It demonstrates why a network should buy it and an audience will watch it.

Another name for a one-sheet is a "leave-behind" because this is the brief document executives often ask you to leave behind after your pitch. You are not going to do that, if you can avoid it, for reasons I am going to explain later. But you are going to create a one-sheet right now so you can further flesh out your idea and enthusiastically present its highlights, effectively and succinctly.

Because people so often ask me for a template for one-sheets, let me immediately clarify that this book is not going to give you fixed templates for anything. That is because different types of shows require specific information to be presented in a certain way. *Top Model*'s one-sheet surely could have opened by selling every girl's dream of being a supermodel, hyping Tyra Banks' involvement in the show then outlining the phases of the competition, all heightened by glitzy images of Tyra and her experts. But *Survivor*'s one-sheet might instead have led with the barren island backdrop for yuppies, presented tribal warfare possibilities then hyped the massive million dollar prize, showing only a picture of a bleak desert island. And your own one-sheet will unfold in whatever manner best sells the strong points of *your* show.

Not to worry! I have never heard anyone say their brilliant pitch was bounced because the network just could not accept their written template. Knowing proper content is a different matter, though, as is knowing how *not to present* information, both of which execs are sticklers for!

To start with the look of your one-sheet, keep as clean a written format as possible. That means no colored paper or text, a single, easy-to-read font in black type, simple headings for any sections and only a few images (and only if those convincingly sell the talent and visual hooks of the show). The written (or spoken) word is what ultimately sells a show. Do not clutter the page with word processing bells and whistles, or execs will be suspicious that your show does not have enough substance to stand on its own.

Now for content. Your one-sheet is your chance to say exactly what this show is and why the network's audience will love it. Unlike a verbal pitch, there is no one to ask unexpected questions, offer a "better idea" for how the show could work before you are done presenting, or just be confused by the opening sentence and tell you to "move on" before you are done fully explaining your amazing concept.

If you thought it was tough to wedge all of your show's essential information into a streamlined logline, the good news is your one-sheet is a chance to expand. You still need the Five Key Pitch Elements. But now you can explain them in great and entertaining detail:

1) The **Who**: You can get far more specific about the personalities and demographics that make your show compelling, comedic and/or unique.

2) The **What**: You can present concrete examples of the types of activities that will take place.

3) The **Conflict**: You can get into psychological detail about why the mix of people, activities and environment is sure to trigger conflict and story.

4) The **Change**: You can pull dramatic, emotional and/or comic strings by presenting the potential change in the subjects who appear on the show and what any prizes might mean to them.

5) The **Eye Grab**: You can describe the various visuals the audience will be treated to and show some of them (don't get carried away with giant, distracting images).

Your one-sheet also gives you the chance to express the tone of the show with your language and writing style. Dramatic, compelling reality TV (like *Intervention*) warrants a more intense presentation; "feel-good" TV (like *The Contender*) should be more uplifting and upbeat in tone; flat-out funny shows can and must have a humorous, edgy feel on the one-sheet.

Remember, there is no correct format for a reality TV one-sheet. Content is king and tone is queen. Here is an example of a one-sheet for *Club Darwin* to give you a sense of one approach. (NOTE: if this were being sent to that network exec I pitched it to years ago, the working title would certainly be changed to his suggestion of *Champs & Chimps*–more on adapting to exec feedback in a later chapter):

CLUB DARWIN

An original reality show
by DMA

We now know there's only a 4% difference between the gene sequences of humans and chimps. What if that 4%...is the poker gene?

TV is drowning in celebrity blackjack, world poker championships, snooker tournaments—get real! Gambling is merely a highly entertaining <u>game of chance</u>. And to prove it...welcome to *Club Darwin.*

Every week, *Club Darwin* pits a team of monkeys, chimps, and orangutans against a team of uptight professional gamblers to see who beats who on the Vegas floor. We're talking hits at the blackjack table, tossing the dice for craps, laying down chips at roulette, and of course, our lovely "Chimpettes," fervently pulling the one-armed bandit in a team slots competition against their hottie human opponents.

Did you know you can train a monkey to scream and clap when coins come out of a machine?

In every weekly half-hour episode of *Club Darwin*, a new team of humans tries to beat the odds—and evolution—in a chimp-stacked casino. Whichever team collects the largest pot at the end of each episode wins. The human winners get money and gifts. The chimps might get pea soup to throw at each other—or the big baby human losers. Whichever way, we'll all get to know monkey and man a little better...and we'll live for the expressions on the human players' faces every time those *&^%$^* screeching knuckle draggers win.

THE *CLUB DARWIN* PLAYERS & STAFF
The Humans—real gamblers, amateur to pro, who take gambling <u>seriously</u>.

The House Team—trained primates who have been cue-captured to respond to the signs of winning or losing (clinking coins, chips being taken away, etc.). No need to dress them; naked chimps up the mock-factor.

The Dealers—led by our main dealer, monkey trainer extraordinaire Surfer Monkey Guy, these are the animal handlers who monitor, protect and cue the monkeys.

The Cocktail Waitresses—drinks are served by more monkeys. Hot ones, of course.

The Muscle—let's consider a trained gorilla. Losers are "bounced" from the floor.

THE POSSIBILITIES
We'll start with the very funny pre-produced "bio packages" that introduce the teams...and finish with "loser interviews" of the monkeys on <u>real</u> entertainment news programs the morning after each show. Add new media blitzes (who wouldn't watch monkeys play slots and celebrate online—or want to play against them?), celebrity competition specials and the requisite "It's a Club Darwin Christmas" album (monkeys can't sing...and that's the idea), and *Club Darwin* is a niche and ancillary goldmine.

Do you instantly understand both the premise and tone of *Club Darwin* as a show? Perfect. Now you are going to craft a one-sheet. Not for your show yet! Write a one-sheet to sell one of your Research Lab shows. Be sure to convey the Five Key Pitch Elements plus the show's tone in two pages or less. As always, feel free to write in this book:

Research Lab One-Sheet

Once you are done with the one-sheet, ask yourself, "Would I buy this? Why?" When you complete your own one-sheet, you will need to hold it accountable to equally strong standards.

But before you can develop your own show further, you absolutely must research what shows like yours already are out there. Hundreds of reality shows have aired on dozens of networks since the boom began, so please do not trust your memory or pop culture awareness to know if your exact idea has been produced or not. Go online and enter key phrases into your favorite search engine (I use Google and quotation marks for speedy searches like, "The Apprentice with chefs"). Check reality round-up sites (Show Starter™ group members, there are links to these on the online group site) and sites for the networks you might pitch to. Talk to friends and co-workers about what shows they loved and hated in your category. Read the trades. Watch reality TV. In particular, watch reality TV shows in the same genre and category as you are pitching.

Now you are saying, hold on a minute... I do not want to be influenced by other people's work! I want to keep things fresh! But you cannot possibly know what is fresh if you do not first learn what has been done or is in the works. And in any pitch meeting, your network exec absolutely will open with: "How is this show different from [show you are afraid to watch]?" If you have watched the show, you will have a short and sweet answer for that. If you have not watched the show, you will have a short and not-so-sweet pitch meeting instead.

You simply cannot walk into a meeting and pitch a show that already has: 1) aired; 2) worse, aired and bombed; 3) even worse, already aired on that network; or 4) run for the hills, aired and bombed on that network, or on the network the exec you are pitching to used to work at before being fired for that particular failed show. Your credibility will be destroyed, and credibility is pretty much all you have in a first pitch.

People also resist studying existing shows because they do not want to be overly influenced and copy another show's format. That is a justifiable concern. If you pitch a show that is too close to an existing one, you will hear the kiss-of-death phrase, "Too derivative." In fact, a few years back, execs would actually say, "If you start any pitch with, 'It's *The Apprentice* but with [different industry here],' I am going to stop you." So how do you find a balance between addressing current trends and avoiding derivative pitches? You need to get original as only the reality industry understands originality to be.

Despite the industry's resistance to derivative programming, people often complain about the lack of "originality" in reality TV. And indeed, it is incredibly hard, and probably pointless, to try to create a show completely unlike anything else in the history of reality TV. You are up against hundreds of hits, flops and staples that cover the gamut of human experience.

In this industry, originality is not about inventing an entirely new genre or category of reality TV! Those are established, with real, trusted production processes behind them. As you develop your first show, instead be sure to highlight at least one of the following Four Original Show Elements in your format:

1) **An original setting.** Move *American Idol* from Hollywood to Nashville and you have *Nashville Star*, a whole new musical, cultural and lifestyle experience for the show. How might a different environment set your show apart from others? Watch out, these can smell very derivative to an exec!

2) **An original cast or talent.** In the endless list of "life swap" programs, reality shows have swapped wives, hairdressers, races, you name it. The lock-em'-in-a-house together fishbowl experiment has been tried with twentysomethings, college kids, sci-fi fanatics, and more. What new subset of people can participate in your show? Or what new conflict-, humor- and emotion-filled life can you explore thanks to your show's central talent?

3) **An original goal or change.** This is where you can have the most fun! For example, home improvement show goals have ranged from duplicating designer rooms (*Sensible Chic*) to decorating your neighbor's

house (*Trading Spaces*) to adding style to teeny-tiny studios (*Small Space, Big Style*).

4) **An original reward.** The industry has offered millions of dollars, new houses, new faces and bodies, (fake) millionaire husbands, million-dollar prizes... What do people in the world want for themselves that reality shows have not yet offered them?

To help you analyze the sellable and original elements of your show, let us examine some of the reasons a network might buy and broadcast *Club Darwin*:

- It brings an original cast, monkey gamblers, to a popular category, Sports & Gaming shows;
- It is visually arresting (by pea soup time, it's "train wreck TV"–for God's sake, it's *Jackass* for monkeys);
- It is funny and unpredictable;
- Monkeys appeal to and/or freak out a broad audience;
- It has endless new media possibilities to connect the audience further to the experience;
- It has unique branding potential;
- The format can be replicated internationally;
- The format can be "spun-off" into other non-gambling areas where humans compete against monkeys (think *Olympic Darwin, Darwin on Ice*, etc.)

With a list like that, I can head into a network office and pitch my original show with pride. But if your research uncovers other shows that are strikingly similar to your pitch, all is not yet lost. Go back to the list of Four Original Show Elements, and rework your show to focus on different original elements than any existing shows already capitalize on.

Now that you have incorporated truly original elements into your show, be clear on why someone should be eager to buy or watch it. This requires more research, too. Want to know the easiest way to know what makes people watch reality shows? Head straight to reality TV fan sites (group members, those links are on our online site, too)! Most networks have forums on their own sites for reality junkies to mingle; those are your greatest tools. If your show is in the vein of *Big Brother*, for instance, read the boards from any season to get a sense of what kept fans hooked. What elements of your show might motivate someone to get up from the couch, turn on their computer and spend hours rehashing an episode with strangers? You now are going to craft a one-sheet around hammering home those strong points in your show.

Open a new document, or grab another piece of paper (your one-sheet will have to be typed at some point, but not everyone can be creative as they type), write the working title of your show across the top, and draft your first one-sheet. I like to talk things through out loud during a first draft because I instinctively will choose elements and language that excite people. Make sure you address all of the Five Key Pitch Elements and at least one of the Four Original Show Elements, and do not edit or censor anything as you write the first pass. If it goes longer than two pages, that is fine, too. Just get your ideas out.

When you are done with the first pass, save it. Now save it as a new file, and re-read it. How can you tighten up the message, reorder elements to sell the gold nearer to the top, or reword language to better convey the tone of your show? Does the one-sheet deliver the same information and feeling as the show inside your head? Remember, you have only one or two pages to wow your reader. If that is too hard to do right now, you may need writing assistance—or you may need to further develop your show idea.

When you are done with your second draft, it is time to take your first pass at your logline (at last!). Try to fully reduce the one-sheet's message and tone into one or two sentences of solid sell!

File both your draft logline and draft one-sheet in your Show File, which now will have five items:

SHOW FILE
- Pitch Database
- Five Key Pitch Elements
- Reality TV Research
- Logline (draft)
- One-Sheet (draft)

You are not yet ready to finalize these documents because you need far more information still. Take another look at all of the elements presented earlier this chapter in *Club Darwin*'s one-sheet. Don't you have a lot of questions yourself about how on earth a show like that could actually be made? And if *you* do, imagine what a network exec is going to ask me in the room! I would have to be able to answer challenges and roll with suggestions as if I had thought of all of those possibilities myself before I ever took the meeting. That means I actually would need to have thought of those challenges and possibilities before I ever took the meeting. And the easiest way for me to do this is create a treatment for the show.

A treatment will help me figure out how to get a show like *Club Darwin* on air, including what it will cost to produce—which absolutely is going to come up in the meeting! (It is going to come up in this book, too, but not right now.) But before you can even begin a treatment, you need to confirm and contractually lock down Key Pitch Element #1: the "Who."

To transform your idea into a sellable show, you must accept and embrace the core reality of reality TV: this is a cast-driven medium. That means a reality TV show is only as good as the people who appear on it. And now, more often than not, those people need a charismatic leader who is the heart of the show! And if that charismatic leader is a celebrity comeback kid from the '80s, all the better. Not joking. Can you say "VH1's Celebreality"?

If you do not incorporate strong central talent, it is going to be nearly impossible for you to sell a show as a first-timer. So let us now take a closer look at the "Who" of your show so you can see why it is the first of the Five Key Elements of an effective pitch.

"REALITY CHECK"

 Pledge #2: I will prepare a pitch and one-sheet for at least one successful reality show I have watched and then do the same for my own idea.

Chapter 5

Steps #4 and #5: Retaining an Attorney and Attaching Talent

There are two reasons for attaching talent to your reality TV show. The first reason is entirely self-preserving. At this point, I hope you understand and embrace that if you do not currently work in reality TV, the industry believes you are bringing nothing, zip, zero, nada to the table in connection with your show. So even if you convince them that your show actually is fresh and producible and they *buy* it, their next step could be to remove you from the show (nothing personal–you've never produced reality before!). But...if you are the one supplying the actual talent for the show, it will be far harder to boot you off of your own project.

The second reason to attach talent to your project is industry-driven. There is serious competition for audience among the networks, so a show that can bring in viewers due to a famous face or a distinctive new talent offers a potential ratings edge (as well as a front person to help promote the show).

At the height of the cutthroat competition genre boom, imagine how many people and companies pitched a reality show for stand-up comics. But when Jay Mohr brought in *Last Comic Standing*, Comedy Central jumped aboard because they wanted to work with Jay Mohr. The same was true for the ridiculously long line of pitches everyone (including me!) was making to create a competitive fashion designer show. Suffice it to say that Heidi Klum's attachment to her version of the show is what gave *Project Runway* the green light–and earned Bravo another runaway hit.

For newcomers, as far as "famous faces" go, if you can get Halle Berry or Lindsey Lohan to agree to do your show, you win, pretty much whatever that show might be. But people who build shows around distinctive, not-famous faces, can win, too (and not go broke trying). Ask the show creators of *Dog, the Bounty Hunter* and *Monster Garage*– your talent does not have to be famous already for you to sell them in a reality show. They just have to be very special diamonds in just the right setting that allows them to shine their brightest. Bling!

As you plan to incorporate talent into your reality TV show, keep an eye out for *two potential danger zones*:

First, do not attach unknown/untested talent just because *you* think they are famous and/or fascinating enough. **Pitchable talent must have an audience, a brand and existing or easily ignited industry heat.** Established production companies that the networks already know and trust can shop their friends and family members as stars of their shows (notice that they still do not). *You* need to come to the table with talent who is at the top of their field and has the credentials and following to prove it (like *The Dog Whisperer's* Cesar Millan). Look, if you have nothing to bring to the deal, why on earth would you attach talent that brings nothing either? They are your ticket in!

Before you pursue any non-famous attachment, first find out who their clients, listeners, readers and/or fans already are and how vocal and loyal they are. You will need that information, at least via written or recorded testimonials, to strengthen your pitch.

As far as stars go, agents are great not just for connecting you to talent, but also for helping you pinpoint who's hot and who's not. Just because someone has been in a movie or on a television show does not mean you can sell a reality show around them, although it does help if at one point they had some kind of developed brand presence (that means *Good Times'* "Dyn-o-mite" JJ might be easier to develop projects for than his straight-man brother Michael).

In the absence of an agent, read the trades and watch reality shows to pinpoint talent trends (visit my "Break into the Biz" blog at www.planetdma.tv for quick tips on reading the trades). For example, surely Flavor Flav's break-out success on VH1's *The Surreal Life* helped another early rap star's show ascend soon after on MTV's *Run's House.*

Now for the second danger zone. Attached talent is only helpful when who they are and what they do is in perfect sync with the show you are pitching. That is considered an "organic" attachment. Do you know how many people have pitched reality shows to, for and about household names like Omarosa and Naomi Campbell–and have not been able to sell them? Just having a recognizable name is not enough. The name has got to be aligned with a complete brand experience, which is still true for Omarosa and Naomi. But the show also has to sell that *same brand experience.* For both Omarosa and Naomi, if the show does not address a "demanding diva" angle–even if the talent themselves resist it–the audience is not going to respond.

Here is a clear example of a show that did not organically match the talent's brand with the show's content. Several years ago, when Oprah-ordained spiritual guru Iyanla Vanzant's own talk show did not succeed, it was not because she had lost her magic touch! It was because the show did not sell the spiritual awareness and authenticity her audience came to her for. You probably can think of other shows that have suffered a similar death-by-bad-branding.

Meanwhile, look what happened when the reality wizards who brought you *The Real World* resurrected Iyanla in full branded "Mother/Goddess" glory on *Starting Over*! Lesson: if you are pitching *Extreme Makeover: Church Edition*, this is not the time to call in your Janice Dickinson "solid" and sign her to the feel-good show of the millennium. You would be wasting a perfectly good brand–and showing

your potential buyers that you do not understand the
industry or your own audience.

> To make it simple, to shop your first reality TV show,
> you not only need sellable **attached talent**, you also need
> a show that seamlessly showcases the talent's brand.

Please believe me on this, as repeatedly confirmed by my
seminar panelists. Pretty much everybody, even established
producers and companies, needs a great talent attachment
to sell a show right now. The difference between the old-
timers and newcomers is that old-timers often have access to
hotter talent and also have the resources and reputations to
tie that talent to a show. Now let me state right now that
not every new reality show you see next year is going to be
helmed by central talent, so no, not every new show has to
be talent-driven. But new shows being pitched by
newcomers to the industry really should be, for the reasons I
shared above. So how do you find talent and commit them
to your reality TV project? Let's tackle this one step at a
time.

Finding Talent
Remember that "talent" is the correct term for the people
who are the central focus of your show. That does not mean
"famous people" or even "performing artists." As you
research and watch more reality TV, track who the principal
characters are in each series. *Dr. 90210* is the perfect fit for
the handsome and charismatic plastic surgeon Robert Rey,
M.D. And the high-rated *American Chopper* is far less about
building bikes than exploring the humorous battleground
that is "Junior" and "Senior's" relationship.
If you really think about it, these shows are hits not
because of the subject matter, but because of the immense
appeal of their main characters and their conflict-ridden,
comedic, utterly relatable daily lives. So for your own show,
it is your job to find a new cast of characters and/or place
them in a new setting that the industry has not yet explored

and, frankly, exploited for entertainment purposes. Now, how do you do that?

You find talent, first and foremost, by paying attention to the people in your life right now, all around you, all of the time. Stop trying to get Pam Anderson's agent on the phone; if she wanted to do a reality show, she would just call Mark Burnett herself. She's *Pam Anderson*. But if your reality show calls for a slightly ditzy caricature of a blonde pin-up girl...is there a real, non-celebrity, fun and funny woman out there with a new edge, who might be even better for your show? Is she, in fact, the over-the-top hair stylist doing your highlights right now as you spam Pam's agent from your PDA?

Here is what so great about your outlandish hairdresser, or your best friend's boxing partner or your neighbor's baby mogul kid. They *know you*. They actually might want to work with you. They actually might appreciate your interest and do what they can to make developing a show for them easier! Again, your brother also might be thrilled to do a show with you, but does he have the professional cred, distinct brand and existing audience you can sell?

If you are in prison, a convent or are just too essentially asocial to have friends or basic personal contacts who can appear on TV, or you just want to explore other options, there are other ways to discover potential talent for your show (or to build a show around). Regional newspapers and local news shows are a huge resource for human interest stories. In big markets, yes, everyone is skimming them for potential finds, but that should not stop you from joining the fray and pursuing interesting people. One of my favorite pitches was perfected by optioning talent I read about in the *Los Angeles Times*.

If you originally come from a smaller town, get online (or on a plane) to check out their local stories, as well. As a native, you have an "in" that mainstream production companies may not be able to break through. And of course, regularly scour social networking Internet sites (like MySpace) and user-generated video sites (like YouTube) where thousands of potentially fascinating subjects join the ranks of the watchable every day.

What are you looking for, exactly? The right talent for your show will have these Five Key Talent Characteristics:

1) **Charisma/appeal/"it."** This is number one because without "it," no one will watch your talent or your show, regardless of how well-executed it is. Whatever made you stop your day and engage with this person (or read their interview), if it makes others do it, too, you are on to something. A great deal of what makes people irresistible is their passion for what they do (think *Miami Ink*). What passion is your talent pursuing–and how can that bolster the mission of your show...or become the basis of a new one?

2) **Big picture.** There are two types of talent in this business: Big Ego and Big Picture. You only want to work with the second! No deal is worth doing with someone who is over-the-top difficult to work with, has outrageous expectations of fame and fortune or cannot make simple decisions for himself or herself, even with the help of representatives. I am writing this generally, but like most other show runners in town, I certainly could name specific talent who have killed projects, shoots and entire business relationships by not seeing all of the possibility before them. When your talent can sit with you and think beyond their dressing room size, their credit, even their weekly episodic commitment, then you have a potential partner in the process.

    One more caveat: If your talent is good-hearted but absent-minded, overbooked or not business- or detail-oriented, know that you will need a dedicated talent handler/producer in your budget to manage the talent's contribution to the show. That requires access to their schedule and contacts (if they are supplying subjects for the show) and cooperation from their support staff. If your talent is willing to turn over some control of their own resources to your producer to keep you on schedule and budget, that is fine (and what I mean by "that is fine" is "get that in writing and that is fine"). If they are not, run.

3) **A distinctive point of view.** You do not need talent who is the only one in the world who does what they do. You just need talent who has put their own stamp on the way they do it. Reality TV has room for endless shows based on fashion designers, for example, because experiencing Isaac Mizrahi's world is wildly different from trailing Vera Wang who approaches life in no way like Donatella Versace. Each would warrant wildly different show formats.

4) **A fan base.** Your talent must have some sort of existing clientele or fan base so the network knows they have a foundation on which to build an audience. If your talent truly is as special as you feel they are, then others will have discovered and confirmed this before you do. And those people also will be a great resource when you shoot your talent reel, as I will discuss shortly.

5) **Talent.** Finally, do not forget that your talent should actually *have a talent* and do it with passion, intensity, humor and a special spark that makes others want to do it, too, or at least watch them do it over and over again. If you have ever seen *Supernanny*'s Jo Frost, you will know why they brought her across the ocean to recreate her British hit rather than recast the show with an American expert.

Do you already have talent in mind–or even somehow attached–to your show idea? Before you proceed with them, hold them up against those Five Key Talent Characteristics. How do they measure up? If it is not a solid homerun in all aspects, get to work on developing them in their weak areas, but also keep your eye out for replacement talent.

Attaching Talent

Having found your show's central talent, how do you now legally attach them to your project? The broad hint here is the word "legally." That means you need a lawyer.

I am not talking here about your college roommate who now practices patent law. Or your brother's old divorce lawyer. **You need an entertainment attorney who**

already has prepared multiple contracts to attach talent to reality shows that have aired.

To keep this section simple, I will just ask if you would even remotely consider reversing the situation. Let us say, heaven forbid, you are married, and heaven forbid even more, you file for divorce. Would you immediately seek out a skilled entertainment attorney to handle your half of the estate? No, that would be *insane.* Even if you and your spouse were only worth $5000, you would hire an expert divorce attorney to protect your rightful $2500.

Well, I am telling you again that selling even a mildly successful reality show is worth $5,000. So any deal you do for your project requires that you hire an entertainment attorney who specializes in reality TV. Not a sitcom or film lawyer. What does a fiction lawyer know about the rights and rewards talent can expect in the less-lucrative market of reality TV? What do they even know of what you yourself can expect in money or credits as a show creator who is bringing talent to the table?

There are several different types of contracts a skilled reality TV attorney can generate to attach talent to your show. I'm just not going to tell you what they are because *I want you to hire a lawyer*.

I am not going to give you a template or form for a talent attachment either, and please do not go online and ask anyone else for one. If you are not ready to hire a lawyer and create solid contracts to protect your show, your estate and your talent, you are still thinking of selling a show as a fantasy or a dream. But television is a business, a high stakes business. And business people have lawyers. Therefore, so must you.

A good non-fiction TV attorney will negotiate a number of items for you in even the simplest attachment agreement, often generically called an "option." Here are some of the areas s/he will negotiate in your talent option:

- Who is being attached to the option?
- What is the project they are being attached to? (You will want to attach a copy of your written format to any contract so that future confusion cannot occur over other shows you or your talent might be involved

in. Aren't you glad you are preparing a one-sheet and treatment as part of the development process?)
- How long is the talent attached to the option?
- Is the talent exclusive to your show during the option period?
- How will talent be compensated, if at all, for the option period (it is perfectly common not to pay for the option)?
- Who will have final say over the format of the show?
- How will talent be compensated, if at all, if the show is sold and produced? (This point alone is worth every dime but one that you pay a real non-fiction attorney.)
- Who owns the show if it does not get sold and produced? (There's that last dime, paying off.)

Please know I am not presenting this partial list to give you a blueprint for cobbling together your own talent option. I am giving you this partial list so you can speak intelligently to potential talent about the kind of issues you two will need to work through as talent considers an attachment to your show.

An industry lawyer will cost you about $150-$500/hour in Los Angeles or New York. Please do not ask them to accept 5% of your show on spec. They are doing tangible work for you and should be paid, and you might never be, even if you sell the show (as I indicated before and will expand on later). Meanwhile, to budget for these initial legal fees, realize that drafting the actual agreement will be nowhere near as expensive as potential protracted negotiations with your talent's attorney. This is where "big picture" talent will serve your project and "big ego" talent could tank or at least jeopardize it.

Of course, I cannot be this firm about your needing an attorney without making it easier for you to actually find one. If you are a member of our Show Starter™ online group, we have provided a "Hot List" of reality TV attorney referrals at the group site to get you started.

Let me add here that if you are developing this show in partnership with another person, you also will need your attorney to draft a contract, or "deal

memo," between the two or more of you. I know, you
are thinking, "We already signed a piece of paper agreeing
to split our millions 50/50!" But sharing intellectual
property involves far more than determining how to divide
the money I already explained you may never see. You will
need to clarify many, many points, like who owns the idea if
the partnership ends, how partners can exit a deal, how the
partnership will be structured, paid, etc.

You do not need to form a production company, LLC,
corporation or other legal entity to shop and sell a show.
Still, you might want to. The best way to decide is: ask your
attorney. Then double check with your accountant.

Once you have met with your attorney, add two more
items to your Show File: your partnership deal memo (if you
are a team) and your talent agreement. Make sure all
parties involved and your attorney have originals of all the
deals.

SHOW FILE
- Pitch Database
- Five Key Pitch Elements
- Reality TV Research
- Logline (draft)
- One-Sheet (draft)
- Partnership Deal Memo
- Talent Agreement

Prepping Your Talent
Once talent has signed your deal (never, ever before! If you
cannot muster the courage to ask talent to sign a deal, you
are going to get spanked in network negotiations, so just
walk away from it all now until you build up the nerve), you
will want to prepare them to potentially join you when you
begin to pitch the project. At the very least, you will need
"tape" on them, which means a talent reel that shows who
they are and how they interact with their audience. If they
are particularly charismatic and interesting, they also might
accompany you to pitch meetings, which can dramatically
help a sale (or utterly destroy it—see "Big Picture vs. Big
Ego" comments earlier in this chapter).

When I pitched *Club Darwin*, I actually had terrific talent in mind for the project. The lead monkey's trainer was a handsome, young, lethally funny surfer dude who worked with trained monkeys and chimps. If I were to have shopped that show seriously, certainly my trainer would have been in the room with me, charming my net execs. Here is what I would have done to prepare him for presentation:

- **Practice pitching.** Get a sense of where your talent really lights up, and where s/he shuts down or gets defensive. Structure your pitch, to include talent only at the moments when talent will sell the show. (More on this in the "Practicing Your Pitch" chapter.)
- **Hire a stylist.** I am not suggesting all talent should be sporting new Manolos or Patek Philippes, just that their hair, grooming and clothes should further emphasize who they are and what that brings to your show. That means something very different if you are pitching talent for *Blow Out* versus *Nanny 911*. A stylist will cost you a few hundred dollars, but the investment could save your show.
- **Fix their teeth.** I am not kidding here. Whether it is $30 worth of teeth bleaching strips or a $400 crown, if it makes all the difference in your talent's look, fix that grill!
- **Explain the process.** Remember that even by reading this book, you are way ahead of your talent in understanding what lies ahead. It is always helpful to manage your talent's expectations of what will happen if the show is sold so they can shift from fantasy-mode to business mentality along with you.

The Talent Reel

To finish up with our *Club Darwin* example, I probably would not have been able to slip a quartet of nattily dressed primates past security at the network for a pitch meeting. But watching Surfer Monkey Guy maneuver those chimps clearly is the heart of the sale. That means I need to produce a brief (5 minutes or less) talent reel to shop the show. (Reality vets please do not skip this section; there is a specific approach I am suggesting.)

To make it simple, a **talent reel** showcases your talent in his or her main environment, interacting with his or her main clientele, achieving the results you are saying s/he will achieve on your show.

For *Supernanny*, an ideal talent reel would show Jo and her magic "naughty stool" taming a wild beast of a child. Surely for *The Dog Whisperer*, the talent reel would feature Cesar performing one of his five-minute behavioral miracles on an out-of-control pet dog. And on *Club Darwin*, Surfer Monkey Guy would have had his monkeys pulling slots, spinning roulette wheels and playing blackjack, screeching wildly on cue every time they won...and gleefully plastering each other with pea soup out of a trophy cup. At least, it looked like that in my dreams.

Another great addition to a talent reel might be testimonials from professionals and clients who have worked with your talent, but only if their industry stature or amazing tales of transformation elevate your talent even further than the personal footage already does.

Beyond content, "production value," or the look, lighting, sound and overall professional feel of your reel, also matters to some extent. Certainly, if you cut a professional-looking reel, it will help buyers understand that you are bringing some skill to the table. But a slick package is nowhere near as important as your talent being able to deliver the goods on tape, those goods, again, being: charisma, a passion, a distinct point-of-view, a motivated fan base and the actual ability to change people with what they do.

Talent reels do not need narration or even sit-down interviews with the talent, though if your talent is particularly appealing, interviews cannot hurt. At minimum, here is how your talent reel should be produced:

- **Use talent's natural habitat if possible**. This not only showcases talent in their prime performance environment, it also keeps them more at ease as they face the cameras. Otherwise, present them in the show's proposed setting, if it is practical (as in, it is not a rented 30-room mansion in Malibu).

- **Shoot on DV or higher**. Do not use home video cameras for the reel because you cannot achieve a professional enough lighting or audio experience. If you can afford it, hire a camera operator to actually shoot it so the tape will look great and you can concentrate on managing the shoot itself.

- **Wire for sound**. Do not rely on a camera microphone for the reel. Your talent's voice is a big part of the package. Get a real mic, preferably a lavalier clipped to your talent, so you have clean audio.

- **Light the set.** Wherever you are shooting, take the time to light it professionally. This is where a good camera operator/director of photography (DP) will pay off. Yes, shooting outdoors will help cost here, but bring along a bounce!

- **Overshoot the experience.** Apart from your talent, the people s/he's working with might be nervous due to the cameras. Shoot long enough that people relax and ignore the cameras. For a reality project, it is critical to see natural-feeling footage of the talent. Extra footage also might help you rework the reel to suit the specific needs of certain networks.

- **Get signed releases from everybody.** Even though this is just a promotional reel, you will want to have all rights to any footage for possible future use. That means your talent and every other person on camera signs an "Appearance" release, any personally owned items that appear in any shots are cleared with signed "Materials" releases, and the location(s) where you shoot are cleared by "Location" releases authorizing you to film them. Finally, the camera operator has to sign a "Work for Hire" agreement, stating that s/he has no rights to the footage. You can get all of these documents from your lawyer. Do not roll a single minute of tape until

you have paperwork signed by everybody.
Preferably, you have gotten it before the day of the
shoot.

- **Edit a clean presentation.** Do not get carried
  away with wedding video spins and dissolves. Open
  the tape with a "slate" showing you or your
  company's name, your talent's name and professional
  title (if that is helpful), the date, the running time of
  the tape, and the working title of the show (if that is
  necessary). You have five minutes for the piece.
  Shoot for three, and lead with your strongest
  material. Definitely add music to sell the energy of
  the show, but do not let it drown out or distract from
  your talent. Finally, end the reel with a title card
  with your name and contact information.
- **Keep the final editing project on disk.** I buy and
  assign a 250-500GB hard drive for each talent reel I
  create. That easily holds a couple of hours of
  digitized footage as well as the final project files so I
  can easily update and edit my reel for customized
  pitches.
- **Dub multiple formats.** Regardless of the format of
  your final master reel, make sure you lay off both
  VHS and DVD copies, and if your editor can do it,
  save a digital file, as well (Windows Media Player,
  QuickTime, Flash, etc.).
- **Label the actual reel clearly and completely.**
  While it is terrific to have a great VHS or DVD jacket
  with graphics and contact information, it is far more
  critical to label the tape or disc *itself* with your show
  name, talent name and contact details. Yes, that
  information is on the reel if it is played; just make it
  as easy as possible for an exec to quickly track down
  your gem in their ever-growing office pile. Once you
  see the desk of a typical net exec or assistant, you
  will understand.

And now...congrats on finishing your talent reel! Be
sure to add a DVD copy as item eight in your Show File:

SHOW FILE
- Pitch Database
- Five Key Pitch Elements
- Reality TV Research
- Logline (draft)
- One-Sheet (draft)
- Partnership Deal Memo
- Talent Agreement
- Talent Reel

Your talent also may want a copy of the reel to file (or to show friends and clients, post on a Web site, add to an existing reel, etc.). That may not be in the best interest of your show, so you may want to wait until after the pitch process to share the talent reel, if at all. Why? You don't want the world to know what you are shopping and with whom, and if your talent is unhappy with any aspect of the reel, they may be less cooperative just when you need them to be the most engaged.

That leads to one last thought on talent. Establish early on what boundaries they have in relationship to the project. Get those boundaries, as gently as you can, in writing with the talent option. For example, talent may or may not have the right to join you in the editing process or even see the final talent reel. They may not be a part of developing the show at all, or they might be an integral part of the creative process. Just establish what they are contributing to the project and keep that line clear. Crazy things can happen when people get a distant whiff of fame. Make sure your talent understands and appreciates that this is a business proposition, and if the show does not sell, that is a business result.

Keep that in mind for yourself, too, if you start feeling a bit anxious or just plain nutty in the pitch process.

Okay, fire up the computer. It is time to create your show.

"REALITY CHECK"

 Pledge #3: I will retain an attorney with a reality TV track record to prepare a deal memo for my partners and me and contractually attach charismatic, credentialed talent to my show.

Chapter 6

Step #6:
Crafting Your Treatment

At this point, you have crafted a basic pitch and developed it into a distinctive, compelling and engaging one-sheet. Your show may have been inspired by a particular talent from the beginning, or you now have identified and attached appropriate talent to enhance your show's impact and further tie yourself to the project.

Now is a great time to rewrite your one- to two-sentence pitch or logline. Incorporate the uniqueness and excitement of your talent (if they are not famous enough to generate that with just the name), as well as the tone and energy from your one-sheet.

Next, recruit a team to test your pitch! Let them read your one-sheet, then run your logline past them. Do their eyes light up...or do their brows furrow in confusion? Keep testing until your team is excited by your one-sheet and even more excited by how perfectly you have expressed it with your logline. Then you are ready to move on. No, not to a pitch meeting! Now it is time to find out if this skyscraper is "habitable." It is time to write your initial treatment.

First, let me emphatically state that this treatment is not for submission to any potential buyer (that is what your one-sheet is for right now). At this stage, your treatment is

to figure out three things:
1) Can this show be produced in a compelling way–or at all?
2) What are the budgeting, schedule, legal and production pros and cons?
3) In what other ways can you expand this show that you have not yet explored?

Writing a treatment at this point not only will help you develop a stronger show, it will give you a chance to uncover and address any questions that might come up in the process of pitching it.

The Treatment

Your treatment is the five-plus-page document that outlines how to turn your brilliant concept into a producible show. Once your pitch and one-sheet effectively present the Who, the What and the Wow, the treatment explains the *How*. Remember that pretty high-rise sketch from Chapter One? Your treatment is the equivalent of a blueprint to construct the building.

To make it simple, a **treatment** is the detailed outline of what your show is and how it will be produced.

Like a one-sheet, there is no set template for how a treatment should be written. Here are some guidelines, though, to help you construct your own:

- Create a simple coversheet (just a title, name and contact information, plus a small image and short, "tag line" catch-phrase, if either helps sell the show)
- Lead with the most potent portion of your one-sheet– the talent, appeal, impact, humor or uniqueness that makes the show exciting and distinct.
- Separate the document into titled sections (sample sections follow), and keep each section succinct and to the point.

Does every show need a detailed treatment? Yes! Remember that reality TV is not documentary TV. You are not just shooting whatever happens in someone's natural setting. You are structuring an experience within a given environment to see how your subjects react. Control over that experience varies from the planned competitions and events of *The Surreal Life* to the seemingly fly-on-the-wall drama of *Laguna Beach*.

No network is going to sign off on a show that is merely a "luck of the draw" multi-week shoot with pretty people and the hope that you can create something spectacular in the editing bay. Even on a show like *Laguna Beach*, you will need to incorporate signpost moments like "Prom Night" and "Graduation Day" into your treatment so you can build story and cast people whose lives will collide with such events (think the "outsider," the "salutatorian," the "partier," etc.).

From strictly regulated competitive formats to loosely controlled vérité docudramas, it is your goal with your treatment to craft a series experience that guarantees some level of conflict and change each show so you can assure the network of story every episode.

Here are the basic sections you will want to include, at minimum, in your treatment (the order they appear in might vary, depending on your show's strong points):

- **The Pitch**

Open your treatment with a tight, compelling redux of what the show is about and who is driving what change.

- **The Show 'Specs'**

Briefly present the technical format of the show. That will include:

Genre and Category: you know this from your pitch database! Is your show a competitive or elimination format, like *Dancing with the Stars*, or a vérité format, like *The Restaurant*?

Episode Duration: Is each episode a half-hour, an hour-long or more? This is not a random decision. Does your extensive content matter necessitate a full hour to unfold, or would it be more effective to hit your homeruns and get out quickly each episode?

Frequency: Does it air weekly, twice-a-week, daily (*aka* a "strip"), etc.? Weeklies often are the easiest to sell because they fit most conveniently into network broadcast schedules. Daily strips are the most brutal to produce or fit into network schedules.

Series/Season Duration: Will your series last for one episode (a "special" or "one-off") or unfold in seasons of 4-6 episodes, 10-13 episodes, or longer? This will be determined by the potential content to be mined from your show's environment or principal cast. Do not panic if you do not have years of material. Reality show life spans are notoriously short; three seasons or more is longevity!

Episodic Format: Does your show feature "arcing" episodes, where the same cast of people populates the entire series order (like *Beauty and the Geek*) or "stand-alone" episodes, where each episode is a separate, self-contained show (like *Flip This House*)? For stand-alone formats, does each episode focus on a single story (like *How Do I Look)*, or is it a "segment show," where several mini-stories make up a single show (like *Cheaters* or *Punk'd*)?

Hosted or Unhosted: The terms "host" and "talent" often are used interchangeably in reality TV. To split vocabulary hairs, though, in reality TV, a "host" exercises control over other participants' experiences on the show, and those participants are the focus of the show. Julie Chen is the host of *Big Brother*. Makeover shows and prank shows all have hosts, as well.

"Central talent" is a person whose personal experience is itself the foundation of the show. *Hogan Knows Best* is an unhosted show with central talent. To go all "high school geometry" on you, all hosts are talent, but not all talent act as hosts.

Shooting Format: Will your show need to be shot single-cam vs. multi-cam, videotaped vs. filmed? Only mention this if it specifically affects storytelling for the show; otherwise, it is an aesthetic and budgetary decision for the production company and network.

As an example of show specs, *Club Darwin* is a half-hour, weekly competitive gambling show, with stand-alone episodes. Every episode, we change professional gamblers, and every season, we will feature a different, ludicrously pimped out casino and add new animals to the fray (trained parrots, cats, etc.). It is an unhosted show, with Surfer Monkey Guy being the central talent.

- **The Cast**

Introduce who will be on the show, including name, picture and a brief bio. Begin with your host if there is one, or introduce the central talent. Then, if there are subjects/participants to be cast, give a short list of what kind of characters and story lines we might see on the show.

　For *Club Darwin*, I would start by introducing my "ring master," Surfer Monkey Guy, what his background is, who his fellow handlers are, and how they will work the different tables at the casino. Next up are the professional gamblers, not by name but by profile (circuit gamblers, online junkies, international title holders, etc.). Then come the primates, by ridiculous name and trained talent. There might be Camilla "Lazy Eye" Gorilla, who can play blackjack with either hand but pelts pea soup most effectively with her right. I would wrap up with the casino staff, various monkeys, chimps and gorillas that will perform funny but functional roles.

- **The Target Location/Lifestyle**

Almost every reality show includes its physical setting as a character in the show, from *The Bachelor*'s mansion to *Nashville Star*'s namesake city. Where is your show set, and how does that setting serve the story? And if your show will be set in your different participants' personal environments (homes, offices, etc.), what types of homes and neighborhoods must you shoot in to advance your show's mission?

For example, *Supernanny* clearly is targeting middle and higher income suburban neighborhoods whose residents have lax-lifestyled, super-mommied and/or double-incomed their way into a tantrum-filled (naughty) corner. In contrast, *Wife Swap* must cast two diametrically opposite households every week. For that show, casting a beachfront modern loft and a log cabin on a lake in the same episode drives story just as much as the people themselves!

For *Club Darwin*, I definitely would get on the phone to lock down at least one casino that is looking for publicity and will sign a letter of cooperation through my attorney. That would be one of the first questions a net exec would zing at me, and it will shift my pitch into warp speed if I can tell them that the Maloof Brothers already have signed on to do the show and are building a new wing with lower slots so even pygmy monkeys can reach the levers.

- **Episodic Breakdown**

To make sure you have enough content for a show, you also want to present what is supposed to happen every episode. Remember, you are not going to create a brand new viewing experience each week! Your audience is returning to your show for the familiarity of the format. They want their "group date" and "private night" and "rose ceremony." Here is where you craft that structure.

To make it simple, work out a sample "clock" for your show. A "clock" is the combination of content and commercials that fills a show's time slot. The typical half-hour clock is approximately 20-23 minutes of programming, usually with three or four commercial breaks. Hour-long shows have about 43-45 minutes of programming, with about six to eight commercial breaks. The show content that airs between commercial breaks is called an "act."

I share all of this so you can see why every act in your show should end with some kind of unanswered question or "cliffhanger" that will bring the audience back after the commercial break. This is simple to do with controlled environments. Makeover shows typically withhold the "reveal" of any change for the top of the next act. Competitive reality shows withholding the final outcomes of games and challenges until after the break.

However, more loosely structured "docudramas" like E!'s *Girls Next Door* are harder to predict. For those, you still will use your initial treatment to generate hypothetical sample episodes to get an idea of what kind of people you will need to book for the show and how many events or locations you will need to plan for to create enough content for one episode.

Beyond outlining the structure of an episode, this section also is where you will list sample episodes to prove you can fill your series order. For instance, for a segment-based prank show like *Girls Behaving Badly*, you would brainstorm at least 20-30 outrageous stunts to demonstrate the endless segment possibilities (or discover that there aren't as many as you thought you'd have!) For makeover shows, you would brainstorm the different subjects you would approach and how they would be uniquely changed by the show. (Hair, grooming and style are pretty much the same procedure each week, which is why so many makeover shows build towards events rather than just a new look. Those events–graduations, first dates, new jobs–are what differentiate one episode from each other.)

This section of your treatment is where you will discover what kind of emotion, humor, conflict and suspense you can build into a predictable structure for each episode, rather than hoping you will strike gold with outrageous cast behavior every week (you won't. No schedule has that much spare shooting time.)

Let's give it a try with *Club Darwin*, shall we? This is a very simple act breakdown for a sample show episode.

Act 1/Event #1–Men and Monkeys face off on the casino floor. There is a coin toss, die roll or some other game of chance to determine who picks the first of the three events: blackjack, the roulette wheel or craps. Then we start Event

#1, which, like all of the events, will be timed. Meanwhile, we introduce our slot pullers, the "Slotty Hunks and Hotties" for the Human Team and the lovely "Chimpettes" for the Primates. They will drink and pull slots throughout the event, racking up final booster points for their teams. As we watch all the players compete throughout Act 1, we also roll "background reels" on both the humans (deadpan serious) and the apes (completely ludicrous). We end the Act just as the players complete their final round at the first table. Time is up on the first event, and our monkey "muscle" collects the chips to see who won the round.

Act 2/Event #2/Monkey Love–While we enjoy "diary" interviews from the competitors, both human and monkey, the chips are counted and announced. We get reaction from the winners and the losers, then it's another face-off to determine Event #2. For this round, the losers also will have to nominate their weakest link to kiss someone from the opposing team. We alert the Slot Teams where their teammates stand and up the drink service. We bite nails through the second timed competition, "Muscles" collects the chips, and we see the pained faces of the gamblers. The Event #2 points are posted, and interviews follow. Someone will have to kiss a monkey in a minute! If the monkeys lose, they will spin a (brand-integrated!) bottle to determine which human they will kiss. If the humans lose, they will nominate their weakest link for the monkey lip lock. We choose our lucky human. Reaction all around!

Act 3/Event #3 and Winners–We kiss and, of course, tell with post-kiss diary interviews. Then it's time for the final event. Either one team is way ahead at this point, or both are neck-and-neck. Event #3 could be the final determination. No face-off this time, just straight to the remaining table for a final, timed round. Chips are counted, points are posted...but it's not time for celebration yet. The Slotty Hotties and Chimpettes join the group with their buckets of shiny tokens. We extract any particularly tempting tokens from the mouths and crevices of the chimps, then those are put into the giant coin machine, too.

Whichever team is ahead gets counted first. Then the trailing team's tokens get counted to see if they can bypass the leaders. We find out who wins after the break.

<u>Act 4/The Prize</u>—If the humans win, they get their cash prize, and the loser monkeys will cheerily shred their consolation bag of peanuts. But if the monkeys win…they get something better than cash *or* peanuts: cold, condensed pea soup. Or refried beans, or something just gelatinous enough to clutch, throw and stick to stuff. Like the humans who lost. (Humans who stick around for the monkey celebration will get consolation prizes that make it worth their horrified while.)

<u>Act 5/Final Interviews and Outtakes</u>—We close the mock fest with bleeped final interviews from our players and outtakes from the day's gambling.

- **The Series Arc**

Recognizing that reality series do not always last more than two or three seasons, project how your series might evolve from Seasons 1-6. This boosts your shot at making a sale by showing how it can come back season after season, with new twists if necessary, and hold an audience. For example, *Survivor* changes location every year, which guarantees a new island with new challenges. Also, in the 2006 season, CBS took a chance by introducing racially divided tribes at the top of the competition. Keep 'em talking!

Explore how you can add a signature to each season of your show while still delivering the predictable punches that keep it popular year after year. *Club Darwin*, for example, would switch casinos each year, add new types of animal stars or even go all-celebrity one episode or season (including the animal players).

- **New Media Possibilities**

Every pitch has to present broadband and mobile possibilities, and that does not mean rerunning clips from the broadcast show. Networks want original content for new media, e.g., *Big Brother's "House Calls,"* and your ability to suggest something innovative here might get you a new media deal for the show even if there is not a broadcast slot for you just yet. Do not overlook new media possibilities! Do a lot of online research for any network that might be a home for your project so you can see what their approach is...and where gaps exist in their online offerings.

    Club Darwin surely could have an online Animal-Cam to watch the show from the monkeys' point-of-view, an interactive gambling area where you could pull slots or play roulettes against a live monkey, and perhaps a personal section where you could read profiles and get to know that special monkey from Episode Two.

- ### Production Budget and Schedule

You will not actually develop a full budget for your initial treatment, but it is important to have a ballpark episodic cost. To do that, you also will need to estimate a production schedule, including: any special pre-production needs (like nationwide talent searches); the number of shoot days per episode (this is extremely important for determining producibility and budget); if multiple episodes can and will be produced simultaneously and why; and how many days it will take to edit an episode.

    We will get into ballparking your show budget in the next chapter, but for now, know that this will be one of the first questions you are asked after you present your initial pitch in a meeting. Suffice it to say for now that *Club Darwin* will not be an inexpensive production!

- ### Brand Integration Possibilities

Keep this short and specific. What you want to present here are opportunities for deep, organic integrations, not generic product placements. The Coke cans in front of Simon and team on *American Idol* are product placements that do not drive story. Leave those out of your treatment. On the other hand, the Denali that *QE*'s Fab Five is racing all over the Tri-State Area in is a terrific deep integration. You would not need to mention the Denali brand specifically, but you definitely would mention that the cast will need an SUV-sized vehicle to cram all of their stuff in and have private team time.

For *Club Darwin*, a key brand buy-in would be from the casinos that hosts the gamblers each episode or season. We will discuss brand integration and its proper scope and liabilities in the budgeting chapter.

- **Format Sales, Ancillary Products and Public Service Possibilities**

Keep this section brief if you include it at all; it can detract from the original show as a focus. Still, if your show cries out to be replicated internationally, twisted into entertaining off-shoots or maximized with distinctive ancillary items, go ahead and think those through here. Again, *Club Darwin* surely should release the *It's a Club Darwin Christmas* CD, and a movie could easily be made with its break-out stars (again, whatever worked for *Jackass!*).

This would also be a good place to mention any banking connections to negotiate a special *Club Darwin* debit card that could be accepted at casinos nationwide. And if there is a public service component that might enhance the network's image and further build audience, address that, too. For instance, the show's monkey stars could do public appearances at animal charity fundraisers.

- **Anything else that matters**

You perhaps consider this a vague statement. You are correct. That is why it is difficult and, in fact, a disservice, to give a hard template for treatments. Different shows will mandate different additional information. For example, the *Club Darwin* treatment would require an entire section devoted to all the research I have done with the ASPCA about the logistics of transporting, shooting and maintaining hygienic premises for that many animals on set. And since this is a gambling show, how will federal and gaming industry regulations affect humans competing against animals? That surely will be a new question for my lawyer.

- ▪ **The Final Sell**

However many sections you develop to crystallize your show, always close with a final sell that wraps up what makes · your show entertaining, gripping and unique.

Down the road, after you get a "yes" on your pitch, you will want to polish this initial treatment more for actual presentation. For instance, you might want to add images (again, small and tone-setting), a brief bio on yourself (if something compelling about you helps to sell the show) and some reference material (again, only if it sells the show—like a *New York Times* front page story on your main talent).
      But remember that right now you are not preparing a treatment for submission. It is strictly for illumination. Yours. And for protection. Yours. Leave images and text you do not have all of the rights to out of this version, the one you now are going to register ownership of.
      Your Show File now should have up to nine items:

SHOW FILE
- ▪ Pitch Database
- ▪ Five Key Pitch Elements
- ▪ Reality TV Research
- ▪ Logline (draft)
- ▪ One-Sheet (draft)
- ▪ Partnership Deal Memo
- ▪ Talent Agreement
- ▪ Talent Reel
- ▪ Treatment

Protecting Your Work
Listen. I truly want you to create fantastic stuff and enjoy the fruits of all of the labor required to do so. But this is Hollywood. Everyone else in the network reception areas, production offices and development meetings around you

has been on a creative bender, too, and trust that some of them have and will, in fact, come up with similar show ideas to yours. So you can and must protect your work. But you can and must also be prepared for someone else to beat you to a sale. And you can and might be ripped off, too, and you will have to come up with quite a lot of cash to accuse a production company or network of stealing your idea and weigh the risk of any possible consequences. That is not to dissuade you in any way from establishing and fighting to the end over your ownership in a show. It is to stay brutally honest about this business.

That being said, whip out your checkbook or credit card! It is registration time.

You have now developed your project to the stage that it legally can be protected. It is no longer "just an idea"! It is a treatment, and you can protect it in two recognized ways. You can register a copyright, and/or you can register it at the Writers Guild of America.

A copyright gives you, the show's creator, the exclusive right to publish or sell your work. It is good for "the life of the author and 70 years after the author's death." Technically, as soon as you put your work into tangible form (like a written treatment), you legally own the copyright. But to give notice to the world that you own it, it is necessary to *register* your copyright. To do so, just complete a two-page Form TX (or one-page Short Form TX, if your circumstances qualify), attach your original treatment with the fee (currently $45) and mail it off to the Library of Congress. It will take several months for them to mail back your date-stamped copyright registration, but it is effective upon receipt of your completed application at the Copyright Office. Simple instructions, more detailed information and all forms are available at www.copyright.gov.

The advantage of obtaining a copyright is that it is the only way to legally offer public notice that you are the owner of your work. Anyone doing a simple title search can find that you, indeed, already have created this format and own the rights. Should they proceed to copy your show, you are in an excellent legal position, with legal standing only a registered copyright affords. However, since it is a public record, anyone can access your copyright submission. Of course, most people do not have the time or funds or online access to descend on Washington, D.C. and pore over millions of records, but it is their legal right to do so.

Your second option is to register, or more precisely, "archive" your work at the Writers Guild of America. Registration is valid for five years. To archive a work at the WGA, you complete their form and submit your treatment together with the fee (currently $20 for non-members and $10 for members in good standing). You can easily do this online by visiting www.wgawregistry.org.

The advantage to Writers Guild registration, apart from the lower price, is that they actually will register even a concept for you, and your submitted materials are not public record. That means no one can access what you submitted in order to steal it, but it also means no one can access what you submitted to verify you created and own it. Per the WGA's site, "The Registry does not make comparisons of registration deposits, bestow any statutory protections, or give legal advice." If you ultimately end up in a lawsuit, the WGA is not required to represent you, but your record of deposit will help establish your creation timeline.

Whichever method you ultimately select, please be sure to register your work and indicate registration on the top page of your work. For a copyright notice, you will type: © "Copyright Year" "Your Name," like © *2006 Donna Michelle Anderson*. And here's a great tip: in Word, just type "(c)" to create the symbol. For WGA registration, you can simply indicate: "WGAw Registered" (for Writers Guild of America *West*). Then you can pitch away knowing you have protected your property. That may or may not prevent someone from stealing it, but you know the saying. If you never put your show out there, no one can steal it...but no one can buy it either. Let me add a new saying to that, courtesy of a wise old fiction TV writer, who essentially says if someone steals your idea, you don't need a lawyer. You need more than one idea.

Your Show File now should have up to 10 items:

SHOW FILE
- Pitch Database
- Five Key Pitch Elements
- Reality TV Research
- Logline (draft)
- One-Sheet (draft)
- Partnership Deal Memo
- Talent Agreement
- Talent Reel
- Treatment
- Registration applications (and final forms)

Shooting a "Sizzle Reel"

Once you finish your treatment, you are going to be very excited about making your show! (If you are not, rework your treatment.) That prompts many people to decide to shoot the show themselves. It gives them a sense of accomplishment, and they often hope to sell the actual finished product. It might surprise you, therefore, that this is not one of the ten steps in the Show Starter™ system. That is because I do not believe the most effective way for you to sell a show is to divert your energy from development to trying to produce a "sizzle reel."

A "sizzle reel" is the common industry term for a short (five minutes or less), produced presentation of your show. Often these are produced for advertisers, particularly during upfronts, and the network pays for them because they already have put the show into development. And certainly producers and production companies will *sometimes* produce a sizzle reel to convey a hard-to-visualize-or-explain element of a show. Here is why you, on a first sale, may not benefit from doing the same:

- **Sizzle reels cannot conform to the expectations of multiple networks.** You cannot possibly shoot a sizzle reel that adapts itself to the different development specs and audience demos of all of the networks you want to approach. So in many of the rooms, your sizzle reel will limit your show's sales potential since it does not match the network's unique brand.

- **Sizzle reels can harm your credibility and divert development seed money.** It takes an enormous amount of money and talent to produce a sizzle reel with the excellent production value a network expects. A less-than-professional sizzle reel will hurt your credibility and divert funds you could be expending on fully developing more sellable shows and paying your lawyer.
- **Sizzle reels narrow a network exec's vision in a meeting.** When you pitch to someone, if they connect to the pitch, they will want to spin it, and expand on it and conform it to their network's particular sensibilities. Pop in a sizzle reel that violates that emerging vision, and that net exec's bubble may burst! The reaction might now be, "Well, that's not what we're looking for." You have to leave room for the network's imagination when you pitch.

If some element of your show requires physical presentation that you cannot effectively demonstrate with excellent writing and core images in your treatment, that is a good reason to consider a production company partnership. Then, at least, you are assuring yourself adequate production funds, infrastructure and experience so your sizzle reel can help sell, rather than sink, your show. I believe, though, that a great show format is truly sellable on the page, in a meeting, and with a strong talent reel. Then let the network finance a sizzle reel if they still need one to fund the show! For instance, I do not need to roll tape of joyous monkeys throwing pea soup at pissed off humans because that description is more than enough to convey my point.

If you absolutely cannot convey the impact of your show verbally, first try hiring a stronger writer for your one-sheet and treatment. Then, if active visuals and/or a complex process are the real sell of your show, and the written word is not doing them justice, develop a budget, hire professionals (including a reality TV producer to conform to norms and avoid copycatting existing formats), and keep the reel short with the powerful punches right at the top. Then make it the eleventh item in your Show File!

SHOW FILE
- Pitch Database
- Five Key Pitch Elements
- Reality TV Research
- Logline (draft)
- One-Sheet (draft)
- Partnership Deal Memo
- Talent Agreement
- Talent Reel
- Treatment
- Registration applications (and final forms)
- Sizzle Reel (only if absolutely necessary!)

All right, now you have a well-crafted pitch, a catchy one-sheet, a compelling talent reel and a well-drafted and protected initial treatment for your show. You are almost ready to pitch! If only...you knew...how much it would cost to make your show. For that, let's move on to Chapter Seven.

"REALITY CHECK"

I will devote real time and research to crafting a solid treatment for the execution of my show then protect it with formal registration.

Chapter 7

Step #7:
Ballparking Your Show Budget

Probably the second most popular question I am asked at every Show Starter™ seminar or private session is "How do I come up with a budget for my show?" The answer is so detailed that we are publishing a separate book in this series to fully address budgeting and scheduling for reality TV. And the process is so detailed that my company soon will release a dedicated software program to automate it since the reality TV production model is so different from the fiction TV and theatrical models current software applications serve.

Right now you are thinking, "Another book! New software? My pitch meeting is next week!" Not to worry. What you need to know about budgeting and scheduling for the pitch phase is far simpler than what you need for development and production. That is what we are going to address now.

In the course of creating your show, you will go through three phases of budgets. The first is your "ballpark budget." This is not so much a line item budget as it is a practical estimate of what it will cost to produce your show. An example of a "ballpark budget" figure is "$85,000 an episode."

> To make it simple, your **ballpark budget** is approximately how much it will cost per episode to produce your show.

Your ballpark budget number lets the network know if your show fits into their budgetary guidelines for reality programming. Smaller cable nets are generally looking for half-hour programming in the $60,000-$150,000/episode range and hour-long programming that is no more than $250,000. At the opposite end of the spectrum, the bigger broadcast nets can often budget shows in the $500,000-$1 million/episode range. But they still would be thrilled to get dynamite shows that fit their brand but cost much less (and can increase their profit margin)!

It is important to research what the budget parameters are for a network before you meet with them so you can pitch shows that they realistically can afford to buy. This makes you look that much more professional in your meetings. If you do not have an agent to get you that information, keep an eye on the trades for any numbers on recent network sales. And if all else fails, when you finally set up a pitch meeting, directly ask the network what budgetary range they are considering right now for new series in your show's genre.

Do not ever simply invent a fake a number you cannot back up in a pitch. Part of the network's question about your episodic budget absolutely is a test of how much you know about this business and what it costs to make a show. Believe me, they will be able to tell from your pitch approximately how much it will budget out at—so your "Jedi mind trick" is to get within a "ballpark range" of that number. We will talk about how you arrive at the figure in one moment.

To wrap up how show budgets progress, your second phase of budgetary bliss launches if your pitch sparks interest at the network level. If so, you will begin cranking out "development budgets." Sometimes you will be paid a small development fee for this; many times, the network will request these for free just to continue considering your show. Until you have a relationship and track record with a network, it will be fairly difficult to get off of the "free budget" circuit. And if the show goes into actual development, you often will have to prepare additional budgets for each revised format you and the net execs · create. These budgets are fully fleshed out, line item budgets that you will need vendor relationships, staffing rates and solid quotes for.

Finally, the third phase begins once the show is sold, when you will start the march towards the final budget for the show. The final budget is key because it establishes the overall "license fee" the network is going to pay the production company to make the show. That figure generally determines what "production fee" or "EP Fee" (for "Executive Producer") the company retains as payment for their services—which is where your payment, if there is one, probably will come from.

Let's return now to step one in the budget-making process, which is estimating your ballpark episodic budget. Now for the surprise insider's tip. **The biggest mistake people make is trying to first create a budget then next develop a schedule that fits that number.** The simple approach is, instead, to rough out a schedule for producing your show based on its logistical requirements, then devise a budget that supports that schedule. This is where the elements of your treatment will serve *and* save you.

If you want a reliable ballpark number for your show, your best bet is to hire an experienced reality TV line producer, ideally from your show's genre, to review your treatment and crunch a number for you. Hello, seed money! This should not cost more than a few hundred dollars, and you might get some valuable tips from them on how to tweak your treatment and save a bundle in production costs. Tempting as it is, do not go to your friend the *film* or *fiction TV* line producer; their production models are different and far costlier than streamlined reality set-ups.

The following are some main treatment elements that will help you and your line producer ballpark a budget. I recommend taking a highlighter and a pen and "breaking down" your treatment on the page for any of these areas that scream "ka-ching!":

- **Show 'Specs'**

Production Schedule: Start with your pre-production phase, which is when you prepare your show to actually be shot. Does your show require, for example, *extensive*: location searches or design; intellectual property clearance; or casting efforts? Talent competitions, for instance, require all three, given the dramatic staging to be built, pop music to clear and performers to audition and select. Any "pre-pro" staff for your show will need to be paid and insured, and travel expenses and materials for a casting team and shooters also might be involved.

Next, once your show is in production, about how many days will it take to shoot everything for each episode? Remember, field expenses for staff, cast and crew rack up for each ten-hour shoot day. To ballpark this, start by counting how many locations you will shoot for the episode. Then, at each of those locations, count how many "set-ups," or separately lit and prepped areas, you will need to shoot. Remember that unlike film, reality usually shoots in the actual order that events take place, so each progressive step of your show often means a new set-up or location.

Here are some rules of thumb to estimate your shooting schedule. One shoot day will accommodate either:

1) **Two locations in the same city with no more than two set-ups at each location.** Your locations should be within a half-hour drive of each other, allowing for rush hour. You can add a "run-and-gun" third location only if you are paying an experienced team, the location is in the same immediate vicinity of a main location and it would not require a lighting set-up. So for a makeover show, you might schedule a clothes fitting and a make-up session in one day, plus an exterior diary session to shoot feedback from

your subject. (Hair is a challenging, long process for female subjects, so that is automatically going to roll you into day two.)

For you non-reality vets, if you do not understand why you should not schedule more than two locations a day, take a break from this book to spend a day in the trenches on a reality show and watch how much time it takes to set up, shoot, strike and relocate a cast and crew.

- or -

2) **Three set-ups in one location.** That means the same house, office, etc. Remember, every time cameras reposition to a new room or area and lights come down and go back up, you have a new set-up. So for instance, on *Club Darwin*, we have one location, the casino, and five set-ups: the Face-Off, Event #1, Event #2, the Slots, Event #3 and the Awards Ceremony. We also are shooting wild animals, so leave some room in the schedule. Our shoot schedule might look like:

Day #1: Face-Off 1, Event #1, Face-Off 2 (at the Event #1 location). We also will need to pay an additional roving team (or mount independent cameras) to permanently cover the Slotty Hotties (another expense!).

Day #2: Event #2, Event #3, Awards Ceremony. Right now, I bet you are asking yourself, um, wouldn't it be easier just to spread this out over three days? Of course! But it not only would cost even more money than the already skyrocketing chimp control fest, it also would be incredibly hard to convince humans to put up with what literally might be crap for more than a couple of days and stay chipper.

For those practical reasons, I had to build a budget protector into my format, which was the timer on the three events, to guarantee how long they would last and protect my two-day schedule. Got it?

Let's finish up our schedule estimate with the post-production phase of your show. This determines how many days it will take to edit each episode—especially if there is a lot of footage to condense into a single show. Many vérité docudramas and makeover shows (over)shoot 100 or more hours an episode then have to condense them into only 45 minutes of story. That leads to a perennial trade-off in a reality budget—do you add story department staff to meticulously pre-produce the shows and screen the footage and transform transcripts into time-coded show outlines (called "paper cuts") for the editors? Or do you keep the story department lean and assign the burden to your editors to filter the footage and carve out story?

Here is a hint. I am not saying the storylines of many reality shows are not cut in the editing bays. I am saying if you plan to do that, you might as well burn five hundred dollar bills for kicks. My advice? Jam-pack your story department staff.

- **Genre and Category**

Competitive formats require additional money to develop games (in fact, they hire an actual staff to do that), *and* they usually include a cash payout or prizes that must be included in your budget. Vérité shows, as we just discussed, shoot an extraordinary amount of footage and require more staff and long editing hours, which affects your budget. Makeover shows need products and services, which you will not always be able (or allowed by the network) to get for free (more on products in a later section!). And it should be no surprise that sports, gaming and travel shows can easily dramatically increase insurance costs. What are the special needs of your genre and category that might trigger higher expenses?

With *Club Darwin*, for instance, both the gambling component (which is heavily regulated by the government and network game show guidelines) and the animal presence (which is heavily regulated by too many institutions to mention, including the ASPCA and the

Health Department) will dramatically drive up the legal, staffing and insurance areas of my estimated budget.

Whatever factors in your format affect costs, remember you cannot jeopardize story and stakes just to bring down your budget...no matter what your line producer says. No one was going to duke it out for weeks on a desert island for 10 bucks, and *The Bachelorette* was not going to work in a cramped fifth-floor walk-up in the meat-packing district! They had to bite the financial bullet and include that mansion in the budget estimate, or story would have been compromised.

- **Episode Duration**

Producing a half-hour show can be just as costly as producing an hour-long version of the same show—but networks do not pay the same fee for both! You will be expected to bring your numbers down for a half-hour show, so be sure to craft episodes that are streamlined enough to be shot in less time. Shortened field production (and the resulting shorter post-production) is where you can trim easy money in half-hour shows.

To keep *Club Darwin* affordable, you will remember I set a timer on the events to limit my shoot days. Creating such a tightly controlled shoot experience also guaranteed the distraction of wild animals on set would be the only unexpected part of the day that could seriously jeopardize our schedule.

- **Frequency**

Remember that ballpark numbers are per episode estimates, whether your show will air once, daily, bi-weekly, or weekly. How frequently a show can air is determined not just by how many days it takes to shoot an episode, but how many days it takes to turn around production and begin shooting the next episode. If multiple episodes can shoot at the same time, that eliminates turnaround, but it hikes up staff and crew costs for separate teams to oversee independent production processes. Your budget trade off here is between

paying more overall production costs for a longer shoot
schedule with safe turnaround time between episodes or
paying more concentrated costs for episodes to overlap
throughout production.

- ## Series/Season Duration

Specials and one-offs can be incredibly costly since they
share many of the start-up, production, post and final
delivery requirements of a full series order. The more
episodes you have in your series, the lower your ballpark
number can be because you will be able to spread fixed
production costs out over considerably more time, or
"amortize" them. *Club Darwin* would be ludicrously costly
for a special, however entertaining; the animal handling and
insurance costs nearly mandate a long episode order. But
your show itself must warrant a longer order, based on its
story and casting potential, before you can up the episode
count.

- ## Episodic Format

"Stand-alone" and "segment-based" episodes have heavier
casting and field production needs (to feed the story machine
that changes every episode), so keep casting and location
demands lean in your treatment. That means you cannot
whittle forty carpentry hunks down to four at the top of
every half-hour home design episode!
   "Arcing" episodes tip the budget in maintenance fees for
the cast you must take care of over multiple weeks, as well
as hidden costs, like the medical and psychological
evaluations, security clearances and follow-up counseling
you might need to provide before you let strangers move into
a house with each other.
   To save costs on *Club Darwin*, it would be critical to cast
one set of animals and pay them out over the series, rather
than try to cast new monkeys every week. It would be
cheaper to pay off the same group of gamblers, too, but that
would hurt story too dramatically. The ballpark has to go
up for that—especially since we need to hunt for gamblers

who will willingly compete against soup-pelting animals (that is a big casting cost!).

- ### Hosts, Talent and Cast

Apart from adding potential union fees, hosts and talent add weekly salaries and maintenance to your budget—as well as agent fees ("plus-tens") if you do not have an alert attorney. More than one host or central talent for your show also requires a dedicated talent wrangler to streamline contact, scheduling, access and publicity demands. *Club Darwin* has a huge potential expense in multiple animal trainer fees, as well as fees for each and every animal on set.

- ### Shooting Format

Your choice of camera and media clearly affects costs for the show. Shooting on DV-cams versus HD, or HDV versus Beta, is a style choice as well as a budgetary one. Media format also might be mandated by the network; for example, some nets require HD delivery to conform to future format requirements (and some provide the equipment and post facilities to facilitate that—which means you do not get those funds for your budget).

How extensively the show is shot also dictates a big portion of the budget. Are you loading sixty cameras into a house and directing and monitoring them around-the-clock? That is equipment, insurance and staffing overload! Or are you taking two basic camera and audio ("ENG") teams into people's homes to shoot them? That adds potential travel, insurance and personally owned equipment or "kit" fees to your estimate.

- ### Union or Non-Union

In general, producers usually budget every show for non-union and battle to make sure the network assumes the difference in costs if it goes union. *Club Darwin* would have its own additional institutional costs due to required ASPCA monitors and guidelines to protect animals on sets.

▪   **Special Needs**

Will special product and service needs for your particular
show affect overall production or even certain episodes? On
a home improvement show, this might include building
permits and contractor's insurance, beyond materials for
actually transforming the location. Or, for example, in *Club
Darwin*, this would include feeding, caging and the Health
Code-regulated cleaning up after at least a dozen monkeys...
who like to fling pea soup. Ka-ching!

▪   **The Target Location/Lifestyle**

There are *three different location options* for your show, all
of which affect your budget differently:
   1) Your first option is to establish one or more fixed
       show locations and bring all of your subjects to them
       (like *Starting Over*). This gives you ultimate control
       over your shoot but generates heavier upfront costs
       for location fees, insurance and set design. Still,
       these you can amortize over the duration of a multi-
       episode order.
           This is, in fact, *Club Darwin*'s one budgetary
       saving grace, that monkey and man taking over a
       single casino actually drives story. Technically, we
       are "caging" the humans in a dimly lit, oxygen-
       pumped, screeching-monkey-filled casino. The
       humans will not be allowed to leave. They will
       gamble with monkeys, stay in luxury rooms on the
       same floor as monkeys, be served drinks and snacks
       by monkeys. Imagine how they will feel the day they
       are released–final diary will be fantastic!
   2) Your second option is to send crews to your subjects'
       locations to film them in their natural habitats (like
       Clean Sweep). Here your budget will take a hit due
       to having to hire and travel in-house crew in order to
       guarantee a uniform and professional feel for the
       show. Or it could spike due to the possibility of
       having to re-shoot footage shot by remote crews who

are not as experienced or familiar with your show, or
due to being held hostage by last-minute location fees
(if you did not get your releases signed in advance) or
by sites that magically fall through the day of a
remote shoot and must be rescheduled on the fly.

3) Your third option is to plan for a mix of fixed and
field locations (like *Little People, Big World*). Of
course, as soon as you shoot for multiple locations,
you run the risk of "busting the schedule" due to
relocation snags. That means you will need budget
protection for overtime and additional shoot days.
But it also means a more interesting visual
experience for your show, which is why most shows
shoot at multiple locations.

So is there a clever (and cost-efficient) way to make one
location feel like many for your show? On a makeover show
my company produced, we took over a two-story downtown
loft and designed every room to be a stand-alone set that
drove story. Because we pre-lit every space during set
design, we were able to shoot three locations day one and
four locations on day two, shaving a full day off of the
production schedule. That mattered for two reasons. First,
obviously, it amounted to 13 fewer days of production, a
huge budget decrease.

Second, and emphatically once again, all budget
considerations simply must be weighed against story
considerations. Makeover shows are exhausting, and it is
incredibly difficult to sustain your subject's interest and
enthusiasm going into day three and four. We chose to
increase the budget to account for keeping dozens of lights
mounted throughout all the months of production, but it was
far cheaper than staffing an additional day of production
and paying location and permit fees so we could relocate
around the city. And our subjects stayed committed and
enthusiastic for the days we were shooting.

- **Brand Integration Possibilities**

It is terrific to identify any branding possibilities that will
enhance the show. What you do not want to do is pre-sell a

product integration agreement before you begin pitching or even assume that free or paid product placements will automatically offset your budget. Sadly, your ballpark numbers cannot reflect potential product integration income. Let me explain.

Brand integration is a far trickier area than most people realize unless they own a production company that has integrated brands before. Let me please debunk the many myths behind the "mother lode" windfalls of placing products on your show.

Remember first how money flows through production companies. Advertisers give moneys to networks, thanks to the efforts of network Ad Sales departments. See the second word in that department title? That's right, Ad "Sales" reps work on commission, just like any other sales person. That means that they have a vested interest in controlling any ad money that comes into the network.

It is very common for newcomers to seek product integration partners to finance their shows before they ever get to a network to pitch. They feel that if their show already is paid for, why would a network not jump at the chance to air it? Here is why.

1) The network might not jump at the show because your contract with the product integration partner gives that company way too much say over the content of the show—which may conflict with the network's programming vision;

2) The network might not jump at your show because that particular partner conflicts with other ad deals in the time slot that is right for your show; or

3) The network might not jump at your show because Ad Sales is irked that you have bypassed their position in the network's infrastructure process and possibly wiped out a potential commission.

Of course, a network may be thrilled if the product partnership is organic and the integration deal language works for them. But that is an enormous risk to take! At most, for your first show, consider researching product partners who will confirm interest in your show without needing a signed attachment to it. This is almost impossible, by the way, since most product companies want to see your network deal before they will consider integrating merchandise into your series. So for a pitch, just make suggestions for integrations and move on.

One final surprise in the brand integration arena. The days of production companies owning or even participating in the money that manufacturers often pay to be featured in shows are over, over, over. Powerful production companies might negotiate some piece of this still. But many production companies never see any of the money for brands that Ad Sales place in their shows. In fact, the network does not even have to channel any of the money those integrations generate back to the show to offset costs! So for all of the work the show's staff has to do to meet the demands of those product contracts, the show itself will not necessarily benefit.

Brand integration dollars cannot figure into your ballpark budget on a first show. Further down the road, when you have some more production clout, this could be a different story!

- **Format sales, spin-offs and ancillary products**

Strike any idea of including this kind of money as a budgetary offset. This is all "back-end" income, which you may or may not get a piece of but will not count towards the actual cost of producing your show.

- **Anything else that matters**

Like that one? This is the hardest area to pinpoint and estimate costs for if you have never worked in reality TV and, especially, if you are not a show runner or line producer who has overseen and protected a real budget. But by now, your treatment should be filled with highlighter color and notes. Just take a look at the clean areas. Are you sure those elements of the show can be done for no considerable additional costs, as in no extra staff, shoot days, insurance, equipment, travel, etc.?

Ballparking Your Show

Okay, you have taken a pass at analyzing the elements of your own treatment that you will need to research or rewrite to ballpark your budget. Because these elements are so show-specific, no one can give you a firm figure for what your type of show is going to cost in general. But I *am* going to present two useful tools you can move forward with.

For your first tool, here are some base numbers for you to begin with then adjust your ballpark according to your treatment notes. Again, your show's particular special elements—for instance, nude pyrotechnics in your final act— can quickly boot you into a different range:

$65,000-$100,000/episode

You are shooting a non-union, half-hour, weekly, vérité series with DV or HDV cams.

You are shooting no more than three locations an episode, all in the same city, with any additional locations shooting as exteriors (each location after the first one moves you closer to the higher end of the range).

You have no separate host and only one central talent and one subject per episode.

You will need no more than two ENG crews a day for the shoot, and you will shoot no more than two days an episode.

Your format is absolutely fixed for every episode; only the subjects are changing.

Children and animals are not part of your show.

Luxury lifestyle trappings are not a part of your show format.

Your target market is small cable nets (like Fox Reality or Fit TV).

$100,000-$250,000 episode

You are shooting the same show above, but it could also be an hour-long format, a segment show, or a competitive format with a small ($50,000) prize.

You require up to five locations (not "cities"; locations) each episode, three of which are distinct interiors. Each location after the second moves you to the higher end of the range.

You have at least two subjects and a host or central talent who are new to the industry (or eager to do the show).

You might have one luxury component that you must budget around (even though this ultimately may be sponsored).

Children or animals may be part of the show but only in supporting roles and not as the main focus of the episodes (unless your central talent truly is the definitive "[fill-in-the-blank] Whisperer").

Your target market is small cable nets for hour-longs or power cable nets for half-hours (like Bravo or TLC).

$250,000-$500,000/episode
You are shooting an hour-long, weekly or competitive or vérité format on DV, HDV or Beta, with multiple locations and/or physical domestic U.S. travel in each episode or a heavily designed permanent studio set.

You are offering substantial combined cash prizes ($250,000+) for competition winners.

You have a recognizable host and/or bankable central cast members who drive the show and will not negotiate lower fees.

There are multiple subjects in each episode but still five or fewer. You have more than three full ENG crews plus, possibly, additional mounted cameras.

You have multiple, varying locations every episode, and lighting is crucial to the look of your show.

You might need to clear at least one intellectual property each episode (songs, film or TV clips, etc.).

Multiple luxury components are included.

Your target market is the top end of power cable programming or the low-to-medium needs of broadcast nets.

More than $500,000/episode
You are shooting a prime-time, union, hour-long, probably competitive format with major combined cash prizes ($500,000+).

There is a high-end studio set with multi-cam shooting, and/or extensive travel, including international, in each episode.

You have a cast of thousands (in reality, that means five or more main people) with multiple story lines to develop, track and shoot every episode in multiple locations.

You have one or more celebrity hosts or central cast members.

You clear multiple intellectual properties (songs, film or TV clips, etc.) every episode.

Your target market is the broadcast nets or a power cable net ready to back a break-out show.

By studying the above information, you should be able to analyze your own treatment, make some big ticket phone calls (e.g., to price out the private jet plane that is central to your story) and devise some more realistic numbers. You also should be able to better explain those numbers if a net exec questions them in your pitch meeting.

If you still are not comfortable committing to your ballpark budget, here is the second tool that we are offering our online group members. Show Starter™ has established a "Hot List" of line producer referrals who will generate ballparks, budgets and schedules for you for reasonable fees. To access the Line Producer Hot List, please visit the Show Starter™ online group site.

Your Show File should now have up to 12 items:

SHOW FILE
- Pitch Database
- Five Key Pitch Elements
- Reality TV Research
- Logline (draft)
- One-Sheet (draft)
- Partnership Deal Memo
- Talent Agreement
- Talent Reel
- Treatment
- Registration applications (and final forms)
- Sizzle Reel (only if absolutely necessary!)
- Budget and Schedule Notes

You now have a logline, one-sheet, treatment and ballpark budget range for your pitch. You are almost ready for your pitch meeting! The last step is to structure the pitch itself and practice, practice, practice it with and without your talent (depending on how you assessed their contribution in the prior chapter). That is because when you go to a pitch meeting, you are not just selling your show. You are selling yourself and the experience it will be to work with you. You cannot control how an exec will respond to your pitch, but you do control what you bring in and must make it as professional and powerful as possible.

Are you ready for the final stage of your pitch prep? Turn the page.

"REALITY CHECK"

 Pledge #4: I will consult with a seasoned reality TV line producer to break down and revise my treatment for a reliable episodic budget estimate.

Chapter 8

Step #8:
Practicing Your Pitch(es)

The greatest thing you can do to move your pitch closer to a sale is to golf weekly with the Executive Vice President of Alternative Programming at a network that is right for your pitch (or with the executive producer of that net exec's favorite production company). If your short game needs work, the next best thing to do is truly know and love what you are pitching and present it passionately and engagingly to your prospective buyer.

That means...*do not wing your pitch!* Practice it so that you are so comfortable with what you have to say that your energy can be focused on the true unknown in the room: how the exec is going to respond.

Also, do not just practice just one pitch and get on the phone to set up a meeting. I absolutely want you to take your applause for doing the hard work on this first pitch. But if you only have one, you are not yet ready for a pitch meeting! If the net exec instantly passes on your first idea, and you have nothing else to throw in the ring, all you will get is an incredulous stare. You have just wasted the exec's time. So while this chapter will give you tips on how to practice your pitch, know that you will need to work through this book's entire idea-through-treatment process for at least three shows because that is the minimum number of distinct pitches you are going to walk into any first meeting with.

To make it simple, you are not ready for a pitch meeting until you have fully developed at least **three distinct pitches** for each potential buyer you approach.

If you already have far more than three fleshed-out pitches, good for you! What you must do before any meeting is select and/or tailor the *top three* that are appropriate for your buyer's brand. That way, if s/he limits your time or number of pitches in the room, you can seamlessly shift gears and begin pitching your hits.

To practice each of your pitches, first revisit the one-sheet and polish it up. Is there any new or compelling information from your treatment that could boost the impact of the one-sheet? Now take a final pass on your logline. Does it sell the Five Key Pitch Elements and convey the true heart of this show? What drives each episode forward, sets it apart from others and entertains and even changes your viewers?

Remember this. At the top of a pitch meeting, your logline's job is to paint as vivid a picture of your show as if the exec were home watching it on a giant plasma screen TV. For instance, I once moderated a Show Starter™ seminar on how to pitch a reality project, and one show runner on the panel recalled a pitch he sold with one sentence, to paraphrase: "It's Mike Tyson...handcuffed...to a different guy each week." That delivers train wreck talent, obvious conflict plus comedy and a visual grand slam in 10 words! But this was not that executive producer's first pitch. There already was trust and a back-nine comfort zone in that pitch room, so nothing more needed to be said until the development contract was drawn up.

If that were *your* first pitch, you might need to shift into explanation mode with a quickness, proving that you had Tyson optioned, what types of guys you were going to cast, what you were going to have them do each episode, how legal issues of handcuffing two humans had been dissected, etc. But in addition to that, far bigger than that, you would need to be prepared for the main reason you are in the room in the first place.

You are not pitching primarily to prove to an exec that you are brilliant, your show is clever, and s/he should love your idea and want to work with you. You are there first and foremost to ring up dollar signs, as in "advertiser-pleasing, sky-high ratings," in that exec's eyes. The entire energy of your pitch has got to focus on why an audience should, will and *must* watch your show. Audiences do not personally know you or need to like you or give you even five minutes of their time, unlike this exec who is trapped behind a desk and has to hear you out. Your passion for making TV, friendly nature and commitment to the project means zero to Bobby Jo in Sioux City. She just wants to be riveted to her television set. How your show is going to achieve that is the mission of your pitch.

And yes, of course, you want the exec to adore you. But s/he can forget your name the next day and still buy your show if it is an audience-grabber.

With all of that in mind, here is what you are going to practice to make your pitch more perfect.

Research Potential Networks
If you are trying to make a sale in reality TV, it is important that you know both the "show" and the "business" side of this industry. In general, that means watching a wide variety of reality programming and checking the trades regularly to keep an eye on *show sales*, *content trends* and *personnel changes* at all of the networks.

Regular reality research will help you develop timely shows and talk about them in a broader industry context when you finally get meetings. It also will help you narrow down which networks are a good fit for your pitch. Identify who is broadcasting shows that have a similar format and appeal to a similar audience as your show. But before setting up a meeting there, be sure to do some deeper research:

1) **Know the network's shows.** If you are not
   familiar with a network's current slate (the shows
   they are developing, producing and broadcasting),
   you are going to sink in "the room" (the common term
   for wherever a pitch meeting takes place). So before
   you pitch, watch at least one episode of each of the
   network's reality offerings.

   Also, get a sense of their production style (high-
   end, generic, bootleg?), the energy of their shows
   (high-energy, life-affirming, butt-kicking?) and how
   they use talent and hosts. Think about what works
   for you on some of their shows so you can incorporate
   that approach into your pitch, *and* so you can speak
   knowledgeably if they compare what you are pitching
   to what they already have on air.

2) **Know the network's upcoming development
   focus.** The shows that currently are airing on a
   network do not necessarily reflect what they plan to
   air in the future! When you first set up a meeting,
   you or your representative (or your insider contact)
   should ask if there is a branding sheet or set of
   development specs the network can send you. If they
   do not (or will not) send one, ask if they can advise in
   what general areas they currently are and are not
   considering content. Remember that only a couple
   years ago, the Game Show Network announced they
   were no longer looking for traditional game show
   pitches and officially renamed and re-branded
   themselves as "GSN"!

   Never skip these first two research steps.
   Otherwise, you might bring *Club Darwin* to Animal
   Planet or National Geographic, neither of which buy
   shows simply because animals are involved. Animal
   Planet's shows tend to emphasize a *harmonious*
   relationship between humans and animals. And
   National Geographic is an action and adventure
   channel!

   The audience for *Club Darwin* most likely would
   be twentysomething guys who love beer and probably
   indulge in other recreational activities and would die

laughing every week just watching monkeys throw canned soup at uptight dudes. So my research would probably lead me to Spike TV or even ESPN if they were actively trying to target a younger male demographic, which, thanks to advertisers, nearly everyone but women's networks always is.

3) **Research the network executives.** It is crucial that you know the names of the manager(s), director, vice-president and executive vice president of Alt Programming, as well as the head of programming, of any network you plan to approach! Trust that these names will come up in pitch meetings. To begin, just go online to the network's Web site and read the executive profiles. If they do not provide them, go online and search "[Network Name]" and "[Title] of Alternative Programming" (for example, "CBS" "Vice President of Alternative Programming"). Be sure to check the date of any results to confirm the information is current! If you must, call the network directly and ask for the names. Just get them.

Next, do a general online search for the exec's bios to see if they attended your alma mater or are from your home town (look for a connection!). Read quotes from trades and personal interviews. Get to know them before you go to meet them. And, as always, database the information you collect, not just for this pitch, but for future ones.

Finally, in the week leading up to any pitch meeting, actively search the online trades for any news at all regarding the specific network you are meeting with. That includes new personnel, new projects, terminated projects, etc. Arm yourself with information!

Research Potential Production Partners

Of course, you may not be practicing your pitch solely for a network meeting. Like many people, you might be planning to pitch to a production company, or even a well-connected show runner, with the hope that they will bring your show to their network contacts. I will explain both of those options in detail in the next chapter.

For now, just know that you will need to do similar research before meeting with a production partner. That includes watching their current shows and getting any programming or personnel updates from their Web sites and the trades. If you have no contacts at production companies to open with, here is some research you can do that can move you closer to a pitch meeting with the right potential partners:

1) **Start with who you know. The simplest way to find a production partner is to approach a company you have successfully worked with before.** You start out ahead because you have some insight to how they run shows, what networks they have worked with and what kind of relationships they had with those networks (as in, if the shows were delivered on time and in a sane fashion). Even better, you have created real relationships with these companies and contributed honest sweat equity to their projects that warrants partnership consideration.

   So as you look through your list of projects, first focus on those you might be able to bring to someone you already know. Even if they do not want to partner on those particular projects, if you have gone through this book and crafted exceptional, well-thought-out pitches, the door will remain open for you to bring pitches back in. They also might refer you to another company they know that might partner on the pitch—and it is more than okay to ask for such a referral.

2) **Identify other production companies your target network(s) work with.** That means *reading the trades* to see what companies are doing deals with which networks. It also means *watching the network's shows* and noting which production company logos are popping up in the end credits—particularly for shows similar in production style to your pitch. Finally, it means *researching online* at the Internet Movie Database (www.imdb.com) to check the company credits for shows currently airing

on the network(s) you hope to reach. It might surprise you how many times the same production company name pops up on multiple shows on a given network (take a look at HGTV's slate and see how many of their shows are produced by the same two top reality companies.)

Warning! Just because a production company has produced a show for a network in the past does not mean the door is automatically still open for them to do another show for that network (executives change, network branding changes, etc.). So when you meet with them, ask if they currently are pitching, developing or producing any shows for the network you hope to sell to. If not, find out who they *are* dealing with now and see if one of your pitch variations might work for that network!

3) **Research the rest of the production company's slate and structure**. Search online and visit the company's Web site to research what shows they have produced and for which networks. That will help you establish if your show is a good fit for their particular expertise and connections. Other areas to explore include: Have they recently produced projects on the scale of your show? Has the company repositioned itself in terms of content? Has the company recently itself split into new satellite companies, or have the executive producers parted ways entirely? You must know who the company's current owners are. That will surely come up in a meeting; in fact, they might actually be the ones you will meet with!

Add potential production partners to your database, too. Even if they are not right for this show, you can quickly access and update the research you just did for future pitches.

As you amass a list of networks and production partners who are a good match for your show, here is the best news: it is perfectly okay, in fact, it is fully expected that you will shop your show to all of them at the same time. Just keep track of who you have contacted and pitched to throughout the process by updating your database and adding that to your Show File (now with up to 13 items!):

SHOW FILE
- Pitch Database
- Five Key Pitch Elements
- Reality TV Research
- Logline (draft)
- One-Sheet (draft)
- Partnership Deal Memo
- Talent Agreement
- Talent Reel
- Treatment
- Registration applications (and final forms)
- Sizzle Reel (only if absolutely necessary!)
- Budget and Schedule Notes
- Network and Production Company Research

Finally, as you start to fill your pitch schedule, be prepared for one common pitfall. Networks re-brand themselves regularly and swiftly. Even your best research cannot completely prepare you for the latest, last-minute edict of what is a great fit for the net. But if you know your pitch extremely well, you can adapt it in the room to respond to any surprises.

The Practice Environment
It is important not only to practice what you are going to say but to be comfortable with where you are going to say it. The number *two* place you will pitch a show will be at a chair on the other side of a desk from an executive. So practice pitching in a mock office, leaning forward, keeping your body relaxed and making great eye-to-eye contact. Then get up and move to a living room! Because in nearly all of the pitch meetings I have been in, and that is literally dozens, I have walked into an office and immediately been escorted to a couch. And there, I have either sat next to or across a low coffee table from, the exec I am there to pitch. And that is a different energy.

Whatever you plan to wear to a pitch, keep that darned low couch in mind. It is not a friend to bunchy blazers, above-the-knee skirts or high heels. Pitches tend to be more casually-dressed affairs, perhaps because of those evil, low couches. Of course, I am 6'1", so this is a particular laugh for all involved at every meeting. But maybe the comfy couch and "pitch uniform" of loafers, khakis and a button-down blue Oxford with rolled up cuffs is all a conspiracy to get you to relax and just entertain the exec with a fun story!

Practicing Your Intro
Take a moment to decide how you plan to introduce yourself in the meeting. That does not mean just your name; it also means how you came to be in the room with this exec. If a contact pulled a personal favor to get you the meeting, verify that it is okay to drop their name on the handshake! Relationships can change very quickly in this business. Whether a well-connected agent or attorney set the meeting up, or you have a particularly pertinent credit you want to establish up top, just think through how you want to initially be perceived at the meeting.

Practicing Your One-Liner
You should know your logline by heart, of course, but sometimes what is wittily written sounds awkward being read off of the page. For instance, *Club Darwin*'s catchy logline of "It's the monkeys vs. man when a team of professional gamblers battles a team of primates on a high stakes casino floor" actually sounds too stilted spoken aloud. So start by reading your own logline out loud and see if it flows like natural speech.

If your written pitch does not yet work as a verbal one, I vote for what I would describe as the "ellipses" logline. That is where you *build verbal story* with brief, dot-dot-dot ("...") pauses. Let's call it "Dragnet" pitching–just the facts, but with an ever-increasing punch.

Club Darwin's Dragnet pitch might be: "We take over a high-end Vegas casino...assemble a team of uptight professional gamblers...then introduce them to their rival team...which is made up...entirely...of monkeys. Then it's just mega-skill versus dumb primate luck to see which team racks up the most chips and wins a weekly grand prize."

With that pitch, I build from the innocuous (the Where) to the ratings-friendly (the Who, intense gamblers) to the visually outrageous (the other Who, their monkey opponents) to the Payoff (competing for a grand prize). I kept the language very simple and fun to sell the playful energy of the show.

But take a show like *Biggest Loser*, and your build will be different because the trump card is different. For that show, the Dragnet might be: "We recruit a bunch of desperate, overweight foodies...strand them on a ranch with two ruthless trainers and lots of temptations...for three brutal months...to compete in teams for perks and completely up-end their diets and lifestyles. Whoever finally loses the biggest percentage of their body weight wins $250,000 as the "Biggest Loser."

For that pitch, the Who is not the ta-dah moment we are building to. Instead, we build from a generic but relatable Who, to an extreme, visual Where, to a Gut-Wrenching What, then wrap up, again, with a zinger Payoff. Language further drives home the "last-chance" energy of the show.

For either show, it is obvious that an audience would be compelled to watch. The big question in the room, however, is...would *the network's* audience be compelled to watch? That is where your research will help. It will tell you what to build to in this one-liner so your exec says, "This is our kind of show."

Now take a look at your favorite pitch on your list and break it down. Of the Five Key Pitch Elements, which are you building to? Start with whichever element is the "innocent" set-up information. Now, what elements offer the distinctive fingerprint of your show? Next, what is the shock value, the twist that grabs an audience? Finally, what is the Payoff that establishes the whole goal of the experience? These can be monetary, like *Big Brother's* winners' checks, or life-changing, like *The Biggest Loser's* weight loss or *Intervention's* detox commitment. The stakes just must be high, dramatic, visual and organic to the energy of the show.

It is great to record yourself as you practice "one-liners" so you can play them back (and not forget exactly how you worded the good ones). If you have a cell phone or answering machine, just use memo mode. Be sure to add these verbal pitches to your Pitch Database, as well!

Practicing Your Pitch
If all goes well, your exec is going to lean forward and say, "Tell me more," or ask a deeper question about your pitch. If you have prepared a thorough initial treatment, there should be no baffled pauses in the room. You will be able to address questions about the ballpark budget (and how you arrived at it, if challenged), where you might want to shoot the show, who you want for talent, the format of the episodes, and much more.

Chances are, though, your exec will simply leave the door open for you to expand on the show concept, and this is where practicing your pitch will save you. Unlike the one-liner, you are going to present your full pitch by starting with the hottest details and working down to the most mundane facts. That is because attention spans are hilariously small in the room and BlackBerrys, assistants, cell phones and e-mail updates threaten to terminate your life support at every second. Open big!

Take out your treatment right now and make some notes on the page. First, where is the eye grab in your show? If your exec asks for more information, start there and say, "What I love, what I can totally picture, is..." Or, if the potentially enormous budget is actually manageable due to some element of the show, sell the budget fix! "The best part is that Cedars-Sinai is actively excited about bringing a non-fiction format into its brand and even signed a letter of agreement to participate. So you may want to work with someone else, but if you are ultimately good with Cedars, they are in!"

Once you pinpoint the high notes of your treatment, practice selling them out loud in brief, bite-sized tidbits to one of your recently recruited team members. If you do not have a partner in crime to join you on this, here is an old acting trick: pick up the phone and speak into it. You cannot help but use natural inflection and enthusiasm when you talk into a telephone receiver. You instinctively know that your voice is all you have to work with, so you use it.

Finally, to use another acting term, it is critical that you get "off book" before your pitch meeting. It is perfectly fine to have papers in hand for reference to more intricate statistics or talent bios. But otherwise boil your show down to entertaining nuggets across your Five Key Pitch Elements so it feels as simple as it is...and memorize it. If the core of your show is too complicated for you to remember, it is too complicated for you to sell.

Prepping Your Talent

If, no, *since*, talent will be a considerable focus in your first show, you also must practice how talent will be presented during your pitch. If your talent is confident, enthusiastic and able to play second chair and follow your carefully constructed lead, and if your talent can easily demonstrate their particular skill in the room, then including them in your pitch is a big bonus. Before you do so, though, walk them through their "nugget" of the presentation and how you will hand off to them.

Your talent cannot open the presentation, but they should be near enough to the top of your program that they are not seat-shifting and thumb-twiddling while you passionately sell. Work with them, too, to make sure you both understand and agree on what part of what they do will have the most impact in the room.

If your talent is a bit strong-willed, is determined to advance his or her agenda for the show or disagrees with how you are presenting them or the show in any way, stop practicing immediately. Work with them on any disagreements to see if their underlying concern can be addressed and achieved through changes to the show format. Remember, unhappy talent is bad, bad, budget-jeopardizing talent. Even if they ultimately get on-board with the final version of the show, have a serious talk with them about how they will behave in the room.

If there is any chance your talent is going to argue with you or undermine your presentation, do not bring them into the room. Of course, you also should reconsider their involvement in your show. Please revisit the chapter on "Attaching Talent" to refresh yourself on why you should work with Big Picture rather than Big Ego talent.

One more caveat: if your talent is late to practice or resistant to the idea of rehearsing, also reconsider bringing him or her to the pitch. It absolutely will not do to have a talent-driven show and have talent arrive at the network half an hour late and/or surly. You should also reconsider keeping talent attached in this scenario because they are going to drain the budget with that approach when you begin production.

If your talent simply cannot accompany you to your first pitch meeting, that is all right. What your exec really needs to see is your talent working magic on a subject similar to those who are supposed to appear on your show. So for all talent-based shows, you need to practice incorporating their talent reel into the pitch.

You should not open a pitch by showing the talent reel because you should be selling a basic conflict and set of stakes rather than just who will be on the show. Talent is your icing. If your talent is wildly famous, of course, you will need to drive home the show set-up quickly so you can get to the reel right away because that is why the exec took the meeting. But do not let talent be the only reason you have a show. It puts you and the show at risk of a short-lived run.

One exception is if you are pitching a vérité show and the talent is the driving force of all of the story. If you are going to follow Danny Bonaduce in and out of home, work and rehab, the network is going to insist on seeing Danny Bonaduce himself to see that he is a willing participant in the madness—and also not a budget-threatening source of it.

To practice the talent or talent reel section of your pitch, identify and rehearse the minimum show elements you will need to establish before amping up your pitch with a talent presentation.

For *Club Darwin*, for instance, I would surely bring Surfer Monkey Guy to the meeting. Before introducing him, though, I would first set up the logline. Hilarity ensues.

Next, I would brandish my letter of intent from the Maloof Boys so the net knows we have eliminated the biggest obstacle to production. I might even address the second biggest concern by saying, "I've also talked to the ASPCA extensively, and we've worked out some great logistics for containing the monkeys on set. And now, I want to introduce you to Surfer Monkey Guy so he can tell you how he came to train his little monkey pals to be ruthless   · gamblers."

Surfer Monkey Guy then would present his practiced rollicking tale of growing up in Namibia and traveling to Kenya for summer safaris. In about 2-3 minutes, my exec would know that Surfer Monkey Guy is spontaneous, witty and deeply devoted to his primate pals. Then I would say to the exec, "Surfer Monkey Guy and I shot a few minutes of serious monkey gambling at the secret Maloof Brothers spa in Reno; can I pop that in? VHS or DVD?"

During practice, please test both your VHS and DVD reels—as in *play them all the way through*. If you cannot sit patiently through your own talent reel, it is too long or dull for an exec to endure. Re-edit.

One important final talent tip: let your talent know that they will only be with you in the room during the pitch of their show. They may not realize you have other shows to present in the meeting, and it can be very awkward figuring out in the room how to get talent out of there and proceed with the rest of your list. So just let talent know that you plan to open with their pitch, and afterwards, you will give them an out to excuse themselves to the reception area. Unfortunately, you cannot let them leave permanently because there is the chance an exec might think up something novel and want to talk to talent again. But at least talent will not be stuck in the room—and possibly distracting from your pitch process—for the rest of your meeting. And since they are out their waiting, it is a good and courteous idea to keep the pitch list for this meeting relatively short.

Practicing Your Goodbye

It is always helpful to have a couple of "exit lines" in your pocket for every pitch meeting. I like to pre-determine a few practical follow-ups I can forward to the exec should they indicate interest in a pitch. For instance, I might say that the Maloof Boys are completing the promo package for the new animal-friendly casino, and I can forward a copy when I get it. Or I might offer to send them a link to a relevant Web site, or even a news clipping with more information they can share when they bring the pitch to a development meeting. For your show, consider what supporting follow-up material you might be able to suggest. Your exec might say no thanks, and if so, you can close with, "Okay, I will just have my rep send over a one-sheet on the show."

If your pitch meeting ends with no bites at all, that is disappointing, but it is normal (which is why a "yes" is such an achievement!). Just wrap up by asking if it is okay to return with future pitches, so you can eventually get that "yes." Have language for this in mind, too! Do not wing anything on a first pitch—you underestimate the brain-emptying power of adrenaline.

Remember that people can completely characterize you in the first five minutes they meet you and often remember you only as you were in the last five minutes before you left. Practice your exit so it feels as smooth, confident and comfortable as your entrance.

"REALITY CHECK"

 Pledge #5: I will extensively research potential networks and production partners so I only bring them pitches that fit their brand. Before I set up a meeting, I will practice every step of my pitch, out loud, to an audience and with my talent.

Chapter 9

Step #9:
Setting Up a
Pitch Meeting

Before you try to sell your project, you first want to get a sense of who your likely buyers are, what the market is, and how to position yourself inside of it.

Remember, there are two methods of distribution for reality shows right now: "broadcast & cable" and "new media." New media distribution, which is primarily broadband and mobile phones, will be addressed in a future volume of this series. If you are not already a member of the Show Starter™ online group, to get on the mailing list for our upcoming new media seminars and training tools, please e-mail showstarter@tidalwavetv.com.

In all likelihood, though, you are reading this book because you have a project that requires the financing, production support, marketing machine and wider TV-screen distribution of a broadcast or cable network. So, again, in this chapter we will concentrate on finding network distribution for your reality show.

Here are the three ways reality TV shows typically get sold:

1) **Established production companies** regularly pitch or are assigned new shows by the networks they frequently work with.

2) When **established show runners** are ready to sell their own shows, they usually are sent out on what I call the "rainbow tour" of network executives, where they pitch new shows to every exec their agent can put them in front of. It is a lot like speed dating, but, hey, it definitely sells shows.

3) There are **all of the other sales** by people with great concepts and/or contacts who ultimately find their way to a network exec's office.

So how do *you* get into that office? The easiest way is to have a top-tier agent who reps reality projects. Sadly, unless you already are a reality TV heavyweight, it can be easier to get directly to a network exec than an agent! The second easiest way is to personally know someone at the networks or production companies you want to approach. So if you work on a reality show, you already are high up on the first-timer's heap. The third easiest way is to know somebody who knows somebody at a network or a production company, and so on...

To make it simple, the easiest way to sell a reality TV show is to **work in reality TV.**

There are only three ways you are ever going to get your reality show out of your head and onto a network screen:

1) Sell it directly to a network;

2) Partner with a production company who will sell it to a network; or

3) Team up with a show runner who will shop it to a network or production company.

Let's take a look at the process, pros and cons of each option.

▪   **Selling Directly to a Network**

Networks are the entities that actually buy shows, so if you can get a great project into the hands of a motivated exec, this is the shortest distance to a sale. Easier said than done, of course, but here is how you can do it.

Get a Reality TV Agent

Many show creators who do not work in reality television launch their sales efforts by trying to wrangle a reality agent to open doors for them. They are frustrated that agents will not meet with them or will not consider representing their show idea on spec. But remember that an agent uses his or her considerable industry connections to get meetings, and they are not about to lose favor with a contact by sending an inexperienced or unprepared client into the room. Also remember that agents are commission-driven, and I really should not need to say again that what you will earn on a sale is comedic, which makes an agent's 10% of "comedic"..."tragic."

So who can get an agent, and how do they do it? Again, this is usually through someone you know, so if you are working in reality TV, talk to your co-workers and bosses to see if they will facilitate an introduction for you. And if you already are at the level of Senior or Supervising Producer on shows, it is actually fine for you to cold call even established reality TV agents. You are one of the new breed of "baby show runners."

Baby show runners actually are hot properties for reality agents right now. There are many Supervising and Co-Executive Producer positions for an agent to fill, and although that does not put a lot of money into his or her pocket, it does get you working that much closer to network execs. And those execs might ultimately buy your shows and package them with loads of the agent's *other* clients!

If you do not currently work at a relatively high level in reality TV, it will be extremely difficult to get an agent. But it is not necessary for you to have one to sell a show! The effort you spend trying to crack a top agency's reality division will be far better spent trying to directly meet network and production company execs.

Work in Reality TV
If you are committed to selling multiple shows and thereby making real money in reality TV, you truly need extensive experience and contacts in the industry. The simplest way to do that is to post your skills on www.realitystaff.com and check their regular updates for job openings nationwide. The odd truth is you will make far more money working steadily in reality TV than you probably will on your first sale. Plus, those paychecks will support you while you are trying to sell your shows, and those credits might keep you attached to a show you finally sell!

If you do not already work in reality, here is a brief primer. Entry-level jobs range from production assistant to researcher to executive assistant for an executive producer. But if you have translatable skills from your current industry, you might be able to work at a higher level. For instance, accountants, bookkeepers and other financial experts can find employment in production offices year-round. Event planners and office managers can apply for production coordinator positions, especially if they have a great contact database that relates to a certain show's mission. Real estate gurus can find work in location departments. And writers and researchers who are savvy online experts might find associate producer gigs in a story department. It can be tough to get that first job—which is why you should look for shows that need your current professional expertise. Given the wide range of reality show subject matter, it is quite possible to find a professional match.

Work for Advancement, Not Security
If you already work in reality TV and now want to sell shows, it is important to expand some of your safety zone to shoot for better job titles and responsibilities as soon as you can. The great thing about the reality boom is that it is relatively easy to rise. That is due to the way most production companies are structured.

As you recall, a show runner oversees each show. And underneath the show runner, a series of producers oversees their own episodes or entire departments. Since show runners often are freelancers with no ties to (or fee participation in) the shows they run, they regularly leave to pitch and helm their own shows. The producers underneath them then rise to replace them. And the staff underneath those producers rises to replace them. That creates the steady "upward suck" of reality TV.

That trend, coupled with freelance careers that expose most reality workers to many show genres, production company styles and network contacts, positions many people to sell shows fairly quickly. And depending on the structure of the production company you work at, you may not even need to be a show runner to deal directly with the network and make those contacts. I first became a network liaison when I was just a story editor on a series.

As soon as you get involved with net execs, take care of them and their current show (rather than instantly try to pitch your own), and they might open a door for you at the network afterwards. Remember, the networks desperately want product; they just do not want to be burned by inexperience and/or show-stifling greed in the process.

One sobering thought for reality veterans who are trying to finally run their own shows. Be aware that you are giving up a great salary for the risky fees of first-time production partnerships or even owning your own production company. I was warned by a show runner I once worked for that I would take a drastic pay cut when I gave up my cushy quote to run my own show. He was right. Still I jumped, and the trade-off was worth it to finally completely manage a show that I had created and had passion for.

Call in a Favor

In the absence of any direct ties to network execs, the next way to gain access is through personal introductions. "Favor meetings" are perfectly acceptable (give a substantive gift to whoever got you in!), but if you work outside of reality TV, be prepared for any executives you meet to be less than excited about hearing your pitch. That is fine; they do not yet know you have read and followed the guidance in this book!

If a personal favor is what got you in the door, you absolutely must wow the exec beyond all expectations. That way, you will either sell a show or get invited back on your own merit (there are few second chances if you come in, as one exec I know calls it, with a "half-baked" pitch). Also, you will not have permanently shut the door for any other referrals your friend tries to make to that exec. When an exec meets you as a favor, there are two possible outcomes: your first impression is either lasting...or your last.

Make Cold Contact (You Schmooze or You Lose)

If you simply do not have any access whatsoever to anyone connected to what is now probably feeling like the world's biggest insider trading scheme, keep hope alive! Come to a Show Starter™ seminar. I often say our industry insider panels don't just offer know-how...they offer know-*who*. You also can take college courses or weekend workshops from executives when they teach. And perhaps the best way to make cold contact with an exec is in their natural habitat. The "industry function."

Because they are always on the prowl for the next break-out shows (read: job-securing and promotion-generating shows), net execs do an alarming amount of industry socializing. They regularly appear on panels, support the various Guilds' events, and sometimes even take their show on the road to professional groups to get the message out about the shows they are looking to buy. Mind you, they accept pitches at virtually none of these events! Come on, they are locked in their offices all day; give them a chance to eat a wedge of Brie.

So how do you get to these functions to meet network execs? You absolutely must be a member of a professional organization to facilitate cold introductions to executives. It does not matter where you live; find out what professional groups in your area serve television producers, and find a way to join, even if you start volunteering for the group or one of the members.

If you live in Los Angeles or New York, you have a number of well-connected professional groups you can join, many of which are listed online at our Show Starter™ group site. To start with, if you work in reality TV, you certainly should join the Television Academy and the Producer's Guild as soon as your credits allow! Both regularly host exclusive events with network execs. And encourage any other professional groups you join to organize a meet-and-greet with network execs (if your group is small, team up with other groups). Make it clear to the executive that your members are coming to learn the right way to approach them about selling a reality TV show, not to pitch.

If you do not live in Los Angeles or New York, to find out who the key professional groups are near you, simply contact the nearest film commission in your region and ask what film and television groups represent professionals in your area. (To locate your film commission, members can visit the database section of the Show Starter™ online group site.)

Contact established professional groups or visit their Web sites to inquire about membership–including what kind of outreach they do or are interested in doing with television industry contacts. Then dip into your seed money to join, and attend events, get to know the members and be a resource for everyone you can. Do not just join and attend one event to get something out of it then blow off the group. People smell an opportunist a mile away, and they will block your future efforts, trust me, especially in a small professional community!

Remember, reality TV is shot worldwide, and even the execs on *The Amazing Race* routinely jump on planes and head overseas to check in on their show. Net execs regularly travel to their show locations across the U.S., as well.

Since these executives would be in your town for specific projects, not to schmooze, one way to meet them might be to work or volunteer on the actual show. To get the word on these gigs, check again with your film commission to see who the established camera operators and other technical crew are in the area because productions often use regional crews for shows. If you have skills you can lend, this is a great "in" to a show. Just remember, the set of a shoot is not the place to corner an executive and pitch! Indeed, it will be difficult to meet the exec at all. But if you do, follow up with a note and inquire into their pitch process then. (Even if you aren't in L.A., pitches are taken over the phone all of the time. You still need to do all of the same steps to prepare.)

Another possibility would be for your professional group or film commission to host a gathering for an exec if they are in town for a while. That way, the exec can discover additional local resources, and local producers can meet them and learn more about what they are looking for. Make sure the event chair specifically asks what the proper way is for attendees to follow up with possible pitches. Then let them eat their Brie!

Seriously, please do not try to surreptitiously pitch a net exec who is out at a function, even if you organized it. It kicks your credibility right in the shins. It says you do not know or care how the game is played. If you get a moment to talk to someone, share with them what you like about their products then ask them what the proper way is to bring them a pitch. They will let you know if they accept cold submissions, agented only, attorney submissions, etc.

Again, if you have no representation and there is no other way to get a meeting, ask if they accept waivers (if you are okay signing one). If they do, they will refer you to a Web site where you can download one. If they do not have an online waiver, request their card and send them a brief thank you note for their time with a brief request for the waiver (provide a fax number, mailing address *and* e-mail address for their assistant).

Warning! Please do not use an executive's card for evil. Evil, if you do not know, is calling a net exec during a work day, ignoring the process they explained to you, and trying to pitch them or tell them about a friend of yours who also wants a meeting. Impress the exec with your own respect, creativity and expertise first, then open doors for others.

If none of these methods works, your absolute last resort is to cold call the executive's office to see if there is any other way to get in the door. Once you do get in, remember that your first network sale does not necessarily mean your first network check! So let me now share the main reason why many newcomers choose not to sell directly to a network.

Know Your Options

In order for a network to buy a reality project, the Executive Vice President of Alternative Programming/Reality Programming or the network President must say "Yes." You, however, will not often meet with the Executive Vice President of Alt Programming. Instead, even if you are somewhat established, you will pitch to a Vice President, a Director beneath that VP, or a Manager beneath that Director. Those three positions all have the power to say one of two things: "No" or "Let me bring this to my boss for consideration." If it then gets a "yes," your reality show is in!

You, however, are not.

Even if you sell a show, if you do not currently own and run an established production company that the network has worked with and trusts, you probably will not get to produce that show.

Note that I did not say you had to be an executive producer or a show runner in order to produce the show. That is because that is not enough. Running a show is crucial experience, but it does not provide all of the business experience you need to run a company. You have to have an actual production company to produce a show. And not one that is a production company because you say so. It is only a production company if the network says so! And they usually will say so only if that company has successfully produced shows for them in the past...or they know and trust you personally.

In other words, just like film studios and their favorite directors, most networks have a "short list" of production companies they are willing to entrust production funds to.

You now are asking, "How do I get on that short list?" Before I answer, let me first explain why networks do and should have short lists. Yes, it is time for another analogy!

For this real-world comparison, let us travel to the world of investment banking. Here, we have Client A, who has millions of dollars to invest in new commercial real estate ventures. So Client A needs to take meetings with various investment banking firms to see who might generate the best return on that money.

Is Client A: (1) going to open their doors to everyone who wants to walk in and pitch a great idea for making money in commercial real estate? Or is Client A (2) going to reach out first to people whose great ideas have generated real profit in the past...and whose great ideas actually can be executed by a real company with all of the contacts and corporate structure to survive the technical, logistical and legal rigors of putting together a commercial real estate deal?

The answer is #2. And, in fact, isn't Client A being savvy and responsible if they skip the open house and simply pick up the phone and call the top three or four investment banking firms in Manhattan, where most of their deals are done, and where their deals have been well-executed in the past? If you were Client A, and that were your money, is that not exactly what you would do?

But wait a minute. What about all of those passionate and enthusiastic investment banking wannabes who read the Wall Street Journal every day and have ideas of their own on how to maximize profit in commercial real estate? Isn't it unfair if Client A doesn't leave their door wide open for each and every one of them to drop by a Vice President's office and offer up possibilities? And shouldn't Client A, upon hearing a reasonably inventive and possibly sound idea, immediately turn millions of dollars over to this total stranger with no training or track record in the industry who cannot even physically execute the transaction with the industry-expected infrastructure?

Well, no. What Client A might say is, "That is a terrific idea—why didn't we think of that?" Then they might call one of their buddies at their favorite real investment banking firm and say, hey, let's give this strategy a try. And everyone is happy...except for the passionate wannabe. They have been unscrupulously cut out of the picture.

Now let's say instead that Client A is a fair and equitable sort of company who loves the idea and appreciates the passion and energy of this new banker wannabe. What is the very best offer Client A can make the wannabe? If you were Client A, what would *you* offer the wannabe in exchange for suggesting a new way to make a deal?

1) A token sum for the idea that Client A now will need to hire an experienced firm to execute;

2) A partnership with one of Client A's top firms to flesh out and execute the strategy, with the wannabe learning from one of the best in the business; or

3) Enough funding for the wannabe to start a new firm, with the title of President, so the wannabe can learn how to actually conduct commercial real estate deals on Client A's dime and perhaps even accomplish it through trial and error?

If you are Client A, the easiest thing to do is just to offer a token sum to the wannabe, which is option #1. But you will only do that if you are legally required to do so. And the last thing you are going to do is option #3, which is to pay for someone else to learn how to do their job. That is what education and work experience are for. Client A is not a scholarship fund; it is a profit-making corporation!

The wisest and most beneficial thing Client A can do actually is #2: partner the wannabe up with a top firm so the wannabe can see how strategies like the one s/he dreamed up actually get executed. That brings the wannabe that much closer not only to one day running a functioning investment bank but also to forging a great relationship with Client A. Wannabe would have to be a self-deluded crackpot not to see the benefits of getting paid on-the-job training with a company that has all of the contacts the wannabe needs for future gigs. Or wannabe just expected to earn big bucks for doing as little as possible. Wrong!

In the case of reality television, the scenarios are no different because TV is a business just like banking. So if Network A has millions of dollars to commission programming, Network A is going to give that to the firms they know will come through with material they can air. And at best, they are going to partner you with one of their "go-to" production companies so your show can be produced while you are getting your trench training. And that is a win-win-win scenario. The network gets their show, the production company gets their fee, and you get your credit for having created a show that actually aired–as well as work experience and contacts for you to move on to future shows.

If you pitch and sell a show to a network, and you do not own and run one of their approved production companies, at the very best, you are going to be partnered with a production company that they trust. Even if you own and run a production company with shows on the air, if this particular network has never funded you, you probably will be partnered with one of their production companies or, at the least, will be handed a show runner that the network chooses to oversee your show.

If a network pairs you up with a production company, it is on you (and your attorney) to independently negotiate a deal with that company to determine your involvement in the show. And this company owes you nothing because the network brought them this deal.

That is why many first-time sellers forge a production partnership before approaching any networks at all. That way, you will have some say over who will be executing the show–and by directly bringing the company a strong pitch, you also have more leverage when you negotiate your involvement in the show if it sells. There are some danger zones here, though, so let's weigh this option carefully.

■   **Partnering with a Production Company**

Consider pitching your project directly to a production company if:
  1) You cannot get a meeting directly with a network;
  2) You have a good contact at a production company; or
  3) You would like a bit more control over your participation in a partnership.

Remember, many networks have a "short list" of the production companies they will actually fund (and can stand to work with). That means you cannot pitch your shows to just *any* production company. During the research phase of this process, you should have identified potential production partners who both produce similar shows and have good track records with suitable networks for your show. Given that it can be far easier to get into the development offices of those production companies than of a network, here is how to take the back-door, production company route to a sale.

Once you've identified two or three established companies that might be a good fit for your show at your target network, contact them directly (if you are a member of our online group, refer to our production company database). You are trying to arrange a meeting with whoever does "development" at the company. At small companies, that is often the executive producers themselves. At middle- to large-sized companies, that is normally a dedicated development executive, like a "Director of Development," or development team. Here are the ways to get in:

Connect through a Personal Contact

Ideally, you have a friend or fellow professional group member who is connected to this production company who can open the development door for you. If you do, that warrants a substantial thank you gift. Not an e-mail with a smiley face or a greeting card. This is a significant gift certificate-level favor someone is doing for you. Even if you do not get a partnership deal out of this first meeting, if you handle the pitch well, you might get in that door again and again with future ideas. Thank whoever opens that door for you with something worth cold hard cash!

Cold Call the Company

If you do not have a buddy doing recon on the inside of the production company, just cold call them directly and say, "I would like to pitch a show to your company; what is the right department or person for me to talk to?" They will either send you to that person's assistant, or they will say they do not take original pitches. Or they will say, and this just stinks, "We only accept agented pitches."

Like many networks, production companies prefer to take pitches through people who are repped by reputable non-fiction literary agents. That is to cover themselves to some degree from charges of idea-stealing by newcomers. If you do not have an agent, it is unusual but still possible to get in through an entertainment attorney. Still, attorneys are for hire, so having one does not necessarily mean you have been vetted for credits and credibility unless it is a top-level reality attorney.

If you have neither an agent nor an attorney, some production companies are happy to take pitches if you sign a waiver acknowledging that many people pitch similar projects and the company itself may already have projects similar to yours in development. If they do not offer this, and you are comfortable signing one, ask for a waiver yourself.

Pitch your Show
Once you get a meeting, pitching to a production company is no different creatively than pitching to a network. You are still there to sell both yourself and the show. You also are there, however, to confirm that this production company currently has deep access to and a good track record with the networks that are right for your show. So to that degree, you also are interviewing *them.*

Negotiate a Deal
If a production company is sufficiently impressed with your pitch to want to partner with you on it, they will offer you a "Deal Memo," which is an agreement that outlines how your partnership will work. Again, this is not something you are going to sign right there in the room or even hand over to your cousin who is in law school to review. You are going to dip back into your seed money, or use up the rest of your current retainer, to have a reality TV attorney negotiate the deal with the production company.

Listen to me. Negotiating deals is standard in business. Do not be afraid of it, and do not be seduced by it. Talk to the production company about what you can contribute to the process and how they see you adding to the experience. Be prepared for them to express little or no need for you at all. That is because they are going to do the bulk of the work to develop this project, they are going to use their hard-earned contacts to sell this project, and they are going to dedicate their experienced production team to executing the show if it sells. They also are going to assume all of the financial risk of delivering this show on-time and on-budget. That means they are going to keep most of the fee the network pays for the show. Do not ask for or expect half of the fee if you do not have the experience to earn it. Again, reality TV is a different world from fiction and film, where selling a project means a guaranteed fee.

There are many other points you and your attorney will want to discuss in this deal, including who owns the show if it does not sell, what credit(s) you will receive that the company is in a position to guarantee, and what, if any, money, you will receive apart from salary for a position you hold on the production staff (based on your experience). Notice that I did not add "back-end participation" (profit-sharing in DVD sales, rerun fees, etc.) since it is still an unusual event in reality TV. You will realize that as soon as you see how happily people give you a piece of it! You should take it, of course, but you really want a piece of the front end if you can negotiate it because that is the only cash anyone is guaranteed to see.

On your first deal, you are not necessarily going to come out on top on paper, but if you can get staffed and participate in production, you will come out on top in the long run. In reality TV, the "long run" is often as soon as your second season or your second show. If you have to choose between a minor development fee and going away for good and a weekly salary and learning how shows are made, take the salary and position! It will be far more money than a payout, and it ultimately will earn you more money regardless of what happens to the show.

Shop the Show to Networks

Once you and the production company have structured and signed your deal, they will take your show on the network road. That might be as simple as a phone call or as intensive as a fully-prepped pitch. You may or may not be a part of the pitch process at network level. Whatever is most likely to sell the show is the best choice for you. Now it is your turn to think Big Ego versus Big Picture. In some instances, if you created a show based on some aspect of your life, you will be a big resource in the pitch meeting because you bring personal experience to the table. In others, you might kill the familiar intimacy the executive producers have with their network execs.

Support Ongoing Development

Another possibility is that the production company may not believe the show is quite ready for presentation. The production company already has seen your pitch, so they know what you have done so far to develop this show (another reason to deeply develop projects before pitching them). If they feel more development is warranted, remember that they are expending their own resources to do this. Volunteer to support the development exec who is working on the show and truly lend a hand to their vision.

In the process of developing your show, the production company may make creative or talent changes that alter your vision and your dream. But the minute you say, "That's not how I want to pitch my show," the good times are going to be over. Realize that you are in a partnership now, and one of the things the production company will have established in the deal memo is who has the final say over creative and financial decisions. That probably will not be you because, again, you do not have the experience or the funds your partner has.

Make sure you are ready to have and to *be* a partner before you sign a deal memo. And make sure your attorney has negotiated an "out clause" for you if you ultimately decide not to move forward with the project for any reason. Sometimes we are so excited to have a deal that we forget to cover our own buttocks. Do not get locked into a multi-year commitment to a show that you can no longer rally behind yet cannot somehow opt out of.

Deal or No Deal

If the production company is not able to sell your show, the reversion rights specified in your deal memo will determine who owns the final format (and can shop it in the future).

If you have no access to a production company partner, a third way to pitch your show is through a show runner. Remember those "rainbow tours"? Not all show runners have their own projects to sell! Here are some tips for meeting and partnering with top reality producers.

- **Team up with a Show Runner**

A third way to get your show into a network for consideration is to work with an established show runner. This is a fantastic approach if the show runner has tremendous experience in your particular show's format *and* has a great record and working relationship with execs at several networks that would be right for your show. That means the show runner might be able to shop the show through his or her own production company, which gives you a production partner and the show runner's company a show. Both of you will be motivated to negotiate a good partnership deal.

If a show runner is not at a level where s/he can form a network-approved production company, s/he will either shop your show directly to networks or bring it to production companies for partnership. That insider connection will increase your chance of making a deal, but now another person will expect a piece of any money from the sale. Of course, if it gets your show sold, it might be well worth it!

To find show runners, go back to IMDb.com and check the names of the Supervising, Co-Executive and Executive Producers on shows similar to your own. Check their other credits, too, to see if they have their own company or have run multiple shows for other production companies and networks (a great sign!).

Show runners can be good partners because they are freelancers who often are looking to establish their own company's projects and brand. They often are represented by agents that can open more doors for you as a team. But does that agency require that you, too, be represented by them in the deal for your show runner to shop the show? Those details and more need to be worked out in a contract before any pitch meetings get set up.

Be very careful before you contractually attach a show runner to your show during the pitch phase. Networks absolutely must approve any show runner on a project, so if they have never worked with yours and do not plan to, you have just killed a possible sale. Do your research!

Your Show File now should have up to 15 items:

SHOW FILE
- Pitch Database
- Five Key Pitch Elements
- Reality TV Research
- Logline (draft)
- One-Sheet (draft)
- Partnership Deal Memo
- Talent Agreement
- Talent Reel
- Treatment
- Registration applications (and final forms)
- Sizzle Reel (only if absolutely necessary!)
- Budget and Schedule Notes
- Network, Production Company and/or Show Runner Research
- Show Runner Deal Memo
- Production Company Deal Memo

Whether you open the network door yourself or your production partner invites you to join them in "the room," the next step in the process is finally the network pitch meeting. Are you ready? Actually, yes, you are.

"REALITY CHECK"

Pledge #6: I will work in the reality industry or join a professional organization to enhance my reality know-how with know-*who*. I will do extensive research before contractually partnering with anyone on my pitch.

Chapter **10**

Step #10:
Pitching Your Show

So either your friend, your representative, your production partner or your scintillating cocktail conversation finally has opened the network door. You are on your very own phone, setting up your very own pitch meeting for your very own project! Or you are on the phone with your show runner or production company's development exec, getting meeting details for your joint pitch. Before you hang up, be sure you:

- Thank them for scheduling the meeting.
- Confirm the date, place, time and approximate length of the meeting.
- Confirm parking details.
- Inquire who you will be meeting with at the network.
- Advise them if talent will be accompanying you.
- Inquire what format is best for a talent reel if you are providing one.
- Confirm your cell number and e-mail address for schedule changes.
- Request a current branding one-sheet if they have one to help you be current with your pitch (if you're dealing directly with the network).

On the day of the pitch, I like to send a copy of my loglines, as well as any prepared one-sheets, to my representatives so they can, for starters, warn me about any pitches that are no longer appropriate (or that resemble a show that was just bought yesterday). Also, if the net exec really likes any of my shows, they might call my rep right after the meeting, before I even turn my cell phone back on. With my loglines in his e-mail inbox, my rep can immediately see what I pitched and speak with knowledge about that show to my potential buyer.

But let's not skip ahead—you just got to your meeting! Right now, you have parked your car 10 minutes ahead of schedule and are waiting patiently in the "holding area" for your net exec's assistant to come retrieve you for the meeting. May I just share some of the behavior I have observed in reception areas that I must urge you not to do?

- **Don't be rude or demanding to the receptionist**. Trust that s/he knows the net exec's assistant and will rat you out in a heartbeat.
- **Don't talk loudly on your cell phone or to your pitch partner**. Too much interruption and information! Bring a magazine to skim, read one of the trades on the table, or prep quietly with your notes or your partner or talent. And be sure to turn your cell phone off when you are called into the meeting.
- **Don't wear sunglasses inside if you are not visually impaired**. You do not look cool, and far worse, you look high. Take off your shades. Donald Trump does not wear them inside, and neither can you.
- **Don't wear a hat inside**. No, it is not the '50s. It just remains unprofessional unless you are Ron Howard or Steven Spielberg and have trademarked the look. You aren't, you haven't, no hats.
- **Don't leave a mess in the reception area.** Please do not leave coffee cups, water bottles and trash in your wake as you follow the assistant to your meeting!

In general, imagine your grandmother is sitting with you and behave accordingly. If your grandmother was an unbridled spirit, imagine *my* grandmother is sitting with you. That will do the trick. If you simply cannot believe I am writing this; if you are, in fact, offended by my condescension, just wait until you get into a reception area yourself.

Okay, you finally are following the assistant back to the net exec's office for your official pitch meeting! Let's deconstruct the coming meeting step by step.

The Introduction

When you meet your network exec, clearly state your full name (they may not even know who they are meeting with–remember how many meetings they take) and thank them for the meeting (no one does this–be original!). Also, if a specific affiliation got you into the room (your agent, your professional organization, your friend) mention it to help the exec know why they should care you are there.

If there is more than one exec in the room, and that person's name is entirely new to you (as in, not one of the execs you researched or any of the people you were told would be there), they should be introduced with their title. If not, find out who they are before you begin. You run the risk of hearing, "Uh, this is the president of the network," so be sure you have done thorough research before you ask! **I keep things simple by asking the assistant when I first arrive, "Will anyone else be joining Network Exec A in the room?"** That also gives you time to call your rep (or your roommate) and get a little background on any additional exec while you wait!

The Small Talk

When you are pitching a network exec, remember that you are one of dozens of meetings that week, and s/he is hoping, fantasizing, but sadly not necessarily *expecting* you to pitch a show that can be brought to the big bosses and get a "Yes." So as much as it is nice to be personable and chatty, know that you are there to knock some terrific shows out of the ballpark. Enjoy some brief small talk, especially if your research turned up common ground, a blurb in the trades praised a show of theirs, four Emmys are displayed on the desk, you are a rabid fan of their product, you are wearing identical outfits (and s/he looks better), etc. Talk about network business only if it is positive and public knowledge, as opposed to, "I just heard your SVP of Alt Programming got fired yesterday!"

What about personal questions? Talk about personal things only to the extent they are publicly displayed in that office. That includes pictures of cute kids and dogs, photos of a recent hiking trip to the Himalayas, etc. Do not ask deeply personal questions or politically risky ones. In fact, break the ice if there is an opening, but truly stay focused on your plan to pitch. The danger here is that the exec settles into a fun chat with you, and the 5-15 minutes s/he had scheduled to meet with you vanishes, and the assistant buzzes in that the next appointment is here.

So have your brief chat, then segue with a direct request like, "I'd love to run three show ideas past you; are you ready for some quick pitches?" Direct requests are good; otherwise, it can be very awkward and time-consuming for both the exec and you to hint your way towards why you are there.

The Set-Up
When you start to pitch, immediately establish how many pitches you have brought and let the exec set any boundaries, like, "I'll only take three today." Then launch simply with "My first pitch is *Catchy Title 1.*"

The Pitch
Open with your one-liner, then pause for a response. If it is just silence, move forward with your fleshed-out pitch, selling the strong stuff first. If it is an instant pass, politely ask the exec to clarify why so you can cross other inappropriate pitches off of the list.

The best way to run a pitch meeting is to be prepared to do the whole show with zero interaction from the exec. That way, there are no awkward silences or uncertain moments. You always know what comes next because you are going to say it. Of course, if the exec takes the lead, that is fantastic, and you can follow along. Either way, relax, deliver your pitches with confidence and a fun attitude (unless a show's tone does not warrant that) and know your shows well enough to adapt them in the room.

Please adapt your pitches in the room. Do not defend the brilliance of your work to the death! If you love it so much, *you* pay for it. (Seriously, Byron Allen became a billionaire off of "time buys.") Otherwise, figure out why the network loves their take on it, and work with them. You can always decide not to sell them the show if the revised version they offer to buy ultimately does not work for you.

Also, if your talent is with you for the meeting, do not forget to release them after their pitch, as you practiced earlier.

Be respectful of the exec's schedule and mindful of the energy of the room. If no limit was set on how many shows you can pitch, ask for permission before launching past your first three. Then just enjoy your presentation. Believe me, they will let you know what their time (and mental) boundaries are!

Now here is one final command: as soon as you get a "yes" on any pitch, you are done with that pitch. *You are done with the pitch.* Simply say, "Terrific! I'll get you follow-up on that first thing tomorrow." Any additional discussion you launch into can only turn that "yes"…back into a "no."

And remember, unless it is the Executive Vice President of Alt Programming or higher, a "yes" in the room only means: "Yes, I will bring this to my boss and champion it as a show we should buy." Which is by no means a development check but is pretty powerful in its own right!

Let's say you just heard, "Yes! I like that one," about one of your pitches (happy dance!). Gauge the room immediately. Is the exec expectantly waiting for additional pitches or happily wrapping up a successful meeting? Consider this. If you pitched more than one show before you got the "yes," unless you have equally knock-out gold bullion on your pitch list, this is a great time to end with a thanks and a smile.

On the other hand, if the "yes" comes for the very first pitch on your list, and you have some additional, well-crafted pitches remaining, select your top two and ask, "Can I run another couple of pitches past you that also might be a great fit?" If those two get a "no," consider wrapping it up and revisiting the exec with the rest of your (refined) pitches another time. You want to leave with the sweaty glow of that hard-earned "yes" all over you–and three or more follow-up bombs will quickly kill the buzz of a winning pitch! Thank everyone and get out of the room as soon as is seemly so you can alert your representative and/or get back to your computer to adapt your one-sheet for submission by the next morning.

The Close
At the end of your meeting, the network exec might ask you for a "one-sheet" or a "leave-behind" for the pitches you presented that they liked. Unless this has been pre-arranged before the meeting, try not to do this. Not because your ideas will be stolen, but because what you came into the room with is rarely the show you and the network exec now have so thoroughly "what if'd." Thank them for their interest and let them know that your rep will send a one-sheet over to them by tomorrow.

By the way, please say "rep" or "representative." If you say "attorney," you will send fire alarms off in their heads. (This is clearly a combative producer! Run!) If you say "agent," that is fine (that is, if you have one), but I say "rep" because it can be far easier to get an attorney to e-mail something the next day than an agent.

At the end of a successful meeting, I like to review the pitches we all agreed I would send more paper on, thank everyone, request business cards and leave the room. At the end of an *un*successful meeting, you might want to challenge the exec to a duel on the rear lawn. Instead, still thank everyone, request a card (and an open door to return) and leave the room. Regardless of the outcome, do not dally at the end (trust that they have another meeting right behind you) unless the exec is happily dallying with you. Just be gracious and go.

The Follow-Up

The day after a meeting, send a brief thank you note to each person who attended (don't gush, just be gracious. Again.). Send any customized follow-up one-sheets you have promised to your rep. Also send your rep the address, e-mail and fax information for everyone who gets a copy (that is what the business cards you collected are for). Do not delay on your follow-up; with all those weekly meetings, execs easily can forget you and your pitch within two days. Note everything you send in your Pitch Database for easy reference. And until you hear back from the network, let your rep check with them once a week or so. No *daily* pressure, but do not let them completely forget about you either (believe me, they can. Nothing personal! Just the sheer volume of meetings and business).

As time passes, I also like to send occasional follow-ups that further the cause of any pitches that got a "yes." If compelling news reports or articles about your topic or talent crop up, send a brief note and one-sentence summary with the information; the exec can use this in a development meeting to further push your pitch.

Ultimately, none of your pitches may have gotten a "yes" from the network executive, or none of the "yeses" may get the green light from the head of programming. That is okay. If you wowed them in the room, you now have officially opened the door at that network to return with future pitches. And that means the possibility of a future sale. Besides, that is only one network meeting, and there are dozens more doors to knock on with your well-drafted reality vision. Do not give up on the first "no"...or the tenth! You will need to rework your treatments to satisfy the brand and audience of each new network you approach...but that is a small task compared to creating an entirely new show.

The other possibility is that you or your rep might get that unbelievable phone call that says, "We're buying the show." Or the production company might call to say, "We sold the show!" Or you might be sitting right in the pitch meeting with your talent and a prayer, and the network exec might say, "Sold." If any of those are the case, congratulations! You have just sold your first reality show!

Aren't you glad you have a lawyer?

"REALITY CHECK"

 Pledge #7: I will be thoroughly prepared for every pitch meeting with a developed treatment, practiced pitch, professional talent reel and upbeat attitude. I will follow up every pitch meeting with a sincere thank you and supporting materials for pitches the network liked.

Chapter 11

The Deal

Great news—the network heavies signed off on your reality show! Now it is time to make a deal.

It was my (unrealized) goal to fit this chapter onto one page. You know why. It is because this is the chapter you and your attorney must write. Signing a deal for a show *without* consulting an experienced reality TV attorney will land you smack in the "Dr. Phil House," wrapped in a straight jacket, with a big, bald Texan scrunching his face at you in disgust. "That dog ain't gonna *hunt!*" he will scream. You will be confused. And I will be confused, as well, if you make it this far in the journey only to cheap out or sell yourself short by not hiring an attorney.

During contract negotiations, you will talk through your attorney and your friendly network exec will talk through a small army of them better known as "Network Business Affairs." All non-legal, creative discussions will continue between you, your production partners and your network executive. But if anyone tries to bypass your attorney and talk legalese directly with you, just say, "You know, I promised my attorneys I would do everything through them, so let me call over there and see if they can get back to you guys right away on this." Your attorney is earning hundreds of dollars an hour to represent you, protect your interests and consult with you on these issues, even though you ultimately will make all final decisions on the contract. So stick to creative development and let them earn their fee.

The deal phase is where some Biz Affairs units deploy the comprehensive "shock and awe" campaigns I mentioned earlier in this book. So here is the second-to-last bit of advice I am going to offer you on creating or pitching a reality show, depending on where you are on the reality experience ladder:

Notes for Reality Newcomers
If you partnered with a production company to sell your show, virtually all of your standing in this sale was negotiated in the deal memo you signed with that production partner. The sale is when "triggers" from that contract will begin, including any money you might receive during the upcoming development phase.

If you instead flew solo in a direct sale to the networks, you have just crash-landed in a sea of sharks. Hey, they are nice sharks, but it is Business Affairs' fiscal duty now to brutally consume any extraneous chum weighing down the show budget ship (um, that's you).

As a newbie, either your talent attachment or your personal experience is going to keep you in the game, or your attorney is going to have to do some very savvy negotiating. You will not be seeing any money any time soon (unless they try to buy you out with a small development check). Remember, though, your goal here is not to make gobs of money but to stay attached to the show and somehow involved with whatever production company they turn the show over to.

You have to stay Big Picture here! This sale is the one thing that can instantly get you production experience, grease the wheel for a second sale that gives you more production experience, and coast you closer to your own production deal.

I like to tell the story of Elise Doganieri, who said to her fiancé one day, to paraphrase, hey, what about a reality show where contestants race each other around the world? Her now-husband, who already was a non-fiction executive producer, developed that show with her then sold it. And on the initial seasons of *The Amazing Race*, Elise, whose idea spawned what is now a legendary reality series, worked as one of many producers on her own show. Many years and Emmys later, she is one of the show runners, but imagine how her staff feels about her for being willing to learn how such a massive show should be produced before deciding she would help run it herself.

One simple thought from this: Whatever is best for your show might actually be what is best for you.

Notes for Reality Staffers

If you have no existing partnership deal memo defining your participation in the show, your attorney still has a far easier time keeping you on your own show because you actually can lend production experience to the game. S/he will certainly fight for a better title than you currently have and some assurances that you can rise towards show runner status over a series of production cycles. Be dedicated and learn from those who are running the show, and it will earn you the respect of your co-workers, bosses and network reps, which will help you rise quickly through the ranks. It also will keep you in the network's and production company's eyes as a potential show runner on other shows.

For that reason, be mindful that you also will need an escape clause should another show sale—or a better-paying, higher-titled job—come your way during this first show's development phase (when you may not be getting paid) or run (when you may be earning, at best, your current rate). Also, keep an eye out for costly exclusivity clauses that restrict you to working only on this show, especially during periods when you will not be making money on the project. Those periods could be development, production, post-production and delivery, unless you actually are on staff for one or more of those stages and will be paid.

Notes for Reality Show Runners

Your attorney absolutely will fight for you to be the show runner on your own show, though you may end up a co-show runner, depending on your partnership deal memo, your experience in this genre, or the clout of any other production company the network brings in.

Your attorney also will fight for your own production company to execute the show. If you have a great track record with the network execs who are buying the show, this could happen, especially if you sold a relatively low-budget show. For higher budget projects, your attorney will fight at least to make the network's chosen production company partner with yours so your company gets its first credit. Of course, if you brought in the production partner, this is something your attorney will have negotiated with that company already.

Your attorney will have to fight even harder to extricate you from utter exclusivity and a long-term commitment to multiple series cycles. But having sold and run your own show is like honey to other network bees, and you want to be able to leverage this sale for more. See what you can do to soften any language that ties you down to one show for years. And if you were able at least to get your production company partnered on this first show, for your next sale, pitch projects with small enough budgets that a network might give your company its own deal.

Making the Deal
Whatever level you are at going into this deal, remember that negotiating a sale can take months. And more months. Months for which you will not be paid but might be expected to do development work because the network has, in good faith, agreed to buy your show. Talk to your attorney about setting boundaries for you, but do not let a tough-talking attorney—or your own greed, empty wallet, entitlement or bruised ego—kill your deal.

A final thought: do not invest tireless energy in trying to own part of the first show you sell. That is not part of the reality business model right now for most people. Mark and Tyra do not own their shows outright (they share ownership with their networks), so know that you will not either. And since you are not the one paying and risking millions of dollars to produce the show, perhaps that is only fair, right?

Maybe. There is a big industry battle going on over format rights, since show creators rarely reap the rewards of their projects being duplicated and lucratively spun-off across domestic and international markets (again, this is not fiction TV!). But know on your first sale, at least, that retaining format rights is a huge demand, and be prepared for considerable resistance from the network.

Do keep financial focus on any money that is *guaranteed* to be paid. Your percentage of any production fee will not be much if you are not the production company who is committing the resources, staff and connections to make the show, but that is only fair, too, right?

Maybe. The production company, if it is the right one, is in a position to gain more from the network for this sale than you might, including the intangible boost of having brought their network contacts another original, sellable show. This may not translate into much money up front for you, but it certainly should translate into other benefits, the least one being a position on the show staff.

Your Show File now will have up to 16 items:

SHOW FILE
- Pitch Database
- Five Key Pitch Elements
- Reality TV Research
- Logline (draft)
- One-Sheet (draft)
- Partnership Deal Memo
- Talent Agreement
- Talent Reel
- Treatment
- Registration applications (and final forms)
- Sizzle Reel (only if absolutely necessary!)
- Budget and Schedule Notes
- Network, Production Company and/or Show Runner Research
- Show Runner Deal Memo
- Production Company Deal Memo
- Network Contract

The Next Step
You already have learned that the next step after having an idea is not pitching it. Instead, there is a detailed

development process to get your show ready to sell. You will not be surprised then, to learn that the next step after selling a show is not producing it! Instead, there is a detailed development process to get your show ready to shoot. That is known as the "Development Phase" of your contract, where you and the network try to craft a solid format and a reasonable budget and schedule for the show. Sometimes you are paid for development, but it is never much (it can be as little as $5,000), especially if you are sharing it with a co-creator—or only getting a small piece of it from your production partners.

The bad news is many shows never make it out of "development hell" into actual production, where producer's fees finally kick in. The good news is most first-time producers do survive development hell and go on to pitch more shows.

Remember, your first sale, just by being a sale, represents capital beyond $5,000, $10,000, $50,000 or even a full production fee. It elevates you to a new position in the industry. It gets you into respected agency interviews where you can be signed and shopped to many more networks without all of the grunt work you had to do to open this first door. It is a passport, a stamp of approval, a membership to a very amazing club. As you have learned in this process, you simply cannot buy that. And it will pay you back handsomely over time if you truly appreciate it...and work it for all you've got.

One last piece of advice for you on this incredible journey. Take a full day and night off and celebrate your first sale. It sincerely might be the last break you take for six months, one year, a decade. Creating and producing reality television consumes your life. It is exciting, surprising, enraging, insane and unlike anything you have ever done. And *that* is why we do it. The money, when it comes, is just a cool extra.

Welcome to the club.

"REALITY CHECK"

Pledge #8: I have finally sold my first show, and my attorney and I are negotiating my network deal. I will read every sentence of the contract myself and ask my attorney to explain everything I do not understand. I will know what I am getting into and, unbelievably, how I might be able to get out of it. I am excited to sell my next show.

Chapter 12

The Final Word

At a Show Starter™ panel I presented earlier this year, a reality producer in the audience stood up and said, to paraphrase, "This has all been so much doom and gloom! Is there any way we're really going to sell a show?"

I really was surprised! It had not occurred to me that it would be depressing or discouraging to lay out the real way reality TV shows are shopped and sold. For me, cold hard facts have always been empowering and inspiring. Yes, I am saying that selling a show is hard. But I also am saying it is possible! In fact, I am hoping to make it more *probable* by giving you the meticulous insider information you need to approach the pitch process in a safer, savvier way.

You truly can sell a show. You just cannot sell one with no effort, money or personal commitment. And once you do it, you may not immediately be rewarded in any way. But dozens of people still do it every year. And I hope you do, too.

I was eight years into a successful reality TV career before I began shopping my own shows and got my first sale. This book did not exist back then as a resource for me. I am proud and excited to offer it now as a resource for you. Please let me know when you sign your first deal.

Appendix A

Seed Money Expenses

Many people hope or expect to be able to sell a show with no money out of pocket. This is possible, but you probably will not stay attached to the show or earn any money from it. If you do *not* plan to give your show away *gratis*, here are some expenses you should anticipate. I cannot guarantee the rates you will be charged; these are **approximations only**:

Typical Expenses

Attorney retainer .... $500+
      (initial partnership and talent option)
WGA or Copyright Registration... $10-$45
Talent Reel .... $250-$1,000
      (camera, lights and audio rental, crew,
      catering, hard drives, editing, dubbing)
Line Producer fee .... $250-$500
      (budget estimate)
Professional memberships... $40-$1,000
      (local groups, Guilds)

Range of typical expenses: $1,050-$3,045

Extended Expenses

Talent Styling... $150-$750
      (hair, make-up or grooming, teeth cleaning,
      teeth whitening, dental bonding, wardrobe)
Sizzle Reel .... $2500-$15,000+
Attorney fees $1,500
      (production company deal memo)
Attorney fees .... $5,000+
      (network contract in the absence of a
      production partnership deal memo)

Range of extended expenses: $4,150-20,750+

Please do not expect to call in favors and shoestring a show sale together. That is not a plan; it is a trap! To be the most effective and protected in this process, you need to pay the professionals who work for you so that *you* determine when and how work on your show pitch gets done.

Appendix B

The "Show Starter" Glossary

This glossary revisits a number of industry terms and concerns that were used throughout the book.

"Kiss-of-Death" Phrases

Here are translations for some "kiss of death" phrases a network or production company exec may say about your show—and what you must do to fix your pitch:

- *It's too derivative.* Your show resembles a popular existing show too closely, with only one differing original element. Add an original twist in a different area of originality (see the Four Original Show Elements, *p. 39*)

- *I don't get it* or *Nothing happens.* Your show, or at least your pitch, lacks a clear mission and does not establish how lives will change due to the show.

- *That show's not producible.* Executing your show is too cost-prohibitive for the budget the show's content and potential audience warrants. Either simplify the show or glitz up the content (like adding celebrity talent).

- *That show isn't castable.* You cannot realistically find enough people with the level of talent, fearlessness or sheer self-delusion your format requires to fill an entire series order. Tone down the demands of the show or make it a special or short-order series.

Basic Teams of Terms

"Reality Players"

Advertisers: The service businesses and product manufacturers who pay to advertise during and in your show.

Brand Integration Partner: An advertiser who supplies goods or services to be featured in a show for free or for a fee.

Networks: The corporations that distribute (air) television shows.

Network Executives: Also called *"net execs"* or *"suits"* (um, not to their faces). The President of Programming and the Executive Vice President, Vice President, Director and Manager(s) of Alternative Programming for a network.

Ad Sales: The network department responsible for deriving and overseeing advertising income for the network.

Business Affairs: The legal division of a network.

Production Companies: Also called *"production houses"* or *"reality houses."* The companies that physically produce reality television shows.

Executive Producers: The owners of a production company and also sometimes the freelance producers who run shows for the companies (*see* "Show Runner")

Show Runner: The Executive Producer (EP), Co-Executive Producer (Co-EP) or Supervising Producer who oversees all assets of production and network interaction for a series. "Co-Show Runner" indicates more than one show runner shares the task of overseeing the show.

******

"Reality Pitching Tools"

Pitch: a one- or two-sentence sales line establishing the mission and key elements of your show. Sometimes called a *"logline."* Also, a written or verbal presentation of your show concept. Also, a meeting to present a show concept.

One-sheet: A one- or two-page summary of what your show is about.

Treatment: A five-page or longer detailed plan of what your show is about and how you will produce it. Also called a *"format."*

Talent reel: A 5-minute or less presentation of your talent that demonstrates their camera presence and ability to do what the show will require them to do.

Sizzle reel: Also called a *presentation reel.* A 5-minute or less presentation of your actual show.

******

The Five Key Pitch Elements

1) The **Who**: Who your host, talent and participants will be.

2) The **What**: The mission your talent or participants will have throughout the show.

3) The **Conflict**: The potential internal and external challenges your participants or talent will face.

4) The **Change**: The potential internal and external change your participants or talent will make, and for what stakes.

5) The **Eye Grab**: The memorable visuals that are signature to your show.

The Four Original Show Elements

1) **An original setting.** A different environment that sets your show apart from others.

2) **An original cast or talent.** A unique talent or new, defined subset of people who participate in your show.

3) **An original goal or change.** A fresh mission for your show's participants to pursue.

4) **An original reward.** Something of impact that people want that reality shows have not yet offered.

The Five Key Talent Characteristics

1) **Charisma/appeal/"it."** The passion your talent has for what they do and how they express that passion.

2) **Big picture.** A long-term approach to a project (as opposed to "Big Ego," a short-term approach).

3) **A distinctive point of view.** Your talent's personal stamp on the way they do what they love to do.

4) **A fan base.** Existing and vocal clients and fans.

5) **Talent.** The ability to do something well and with enough passion to make others want to watch them do it.

Appendix C

The Reality Check List

Pledge #1: I will read and apply the entire Show Starter™ system, without skipping any chapters, steps or exercises, before I attempt to sell my first show.

Pledge #2: I will prepare a pitch and one-sheet for at least one successful reality show I have watched and then do the same for my own idea.

Pledge #3: I will retain an attorney with a reality TV track record to prepare a deal memo for my partners and me and contractually attach charismatic, credentialed talent to my show.

Pledge #4: I will consult with a seasoned reality TV line producer to break down and revise my treatment for a reliable episodic budget estimate.

Pledge #5: I will extensively research potential networks and production partners so I only bring them pitches that fit their brand. Before I set up a meeting, I will practice every step of my pitch, out loud, to an audience and with my talent.

Pledge #6: I will obtain work in the reality industry or join a professional organization to attend and organize networking events to enhance my reality know-how with know-*who*.

Pledge #7: I will be thoroughly prepared for every pitch meeting with a developed treatment, practiced pitch, professional talent reel and upbeat attitude. I will follow up every pitch meeting with a sincere thank you and supporting materials for pitches the network liked.

Pledge #8: I have finally sold my first show, and my attorney and I are negotiating my network deal. I will read every sentence of the contract myself and ask my attorney to explain everything I do not yet understand. I will know what I am getting into and, unbelievably, how I might be able to get out of it. I am excited to sell my next show.

About the Author

For 10 years, Donna Michelle Anderson, p/k/a "DMA," has been a successful writer, producer and show runner of dozens of highly rated non-fiction television programs for such networks as CBS, UPN, Fox, Bravo, BET, History Channel, TLC, and more. She is executive producer of non-fiction and new media production company Tidal Wave TV in Los Angeles.

Since 2002, DMA also has been the director of the Movie in a Box one-day filmmaking seminars. The seminars bring hit movie makers such as Miguel Arteta (*The Good Girl*) and Effie Brown (*Real Women Have Curves*) off of the set and into the classroom, alongside top industry vendors. The featured screenwriting program is her "1-3-5 Story Structure Made Simple System." DMA, a former story analyst at a major Hollywood production company, has taught the popular system to students at the prestigious UCLA Extension Writing Program and colleges, film festivals, industry conferences and private clients across the country.

In 2006, DMA launched "Planet DMA," a public speaking and training experience offering practical insider tools to realizing goals inside and beyond the entertainment industry. Her first book, "The 1-3-5 Story Structure Made Simple System: The Nine Essential Elements of a Sellable Screenplay" was published in May 2006 by Movie in a Box Books. It was followed by Tidal Wave TV's first broadband series, "Hollywood Calls™," an online call-in show that answers people's questions about how to break into the biz (airing on www.planetdma.tv). In the same year, Tidal Wave TV also formalized its Show Starter™ production services arm, to continue setting up shows for existing companies and new producers and to offer reality show seminars and training for organizations such as the Producers Guild of America, the Writers Guild of America's and Stanford in Entertainment.

DMA is an active member of the Academy of Television Arts & Sciences, the Producers Guild of America and Mensans in Showbiz. She graduated with honors from Stanford University.

Please visit the Show Starter™ Web site to take advantage of all of our "Reality Production Instruction" products and services:

www.tidalwavetv.com/ShowStarter

SHOW STARTER™ Seminars offer individual and group training on how to sell and set up non-fiction shows.

SHOW STARTER™ Services let you outsource pre-production, just like you already do with post!

SHOW STARTER™ Consultations offer private, individual services for your project.

Buy these titles now from
Movie in a Box Books!

And look for these upcoming titles in the
Show Starter™ Reality TV Made Simple series:

- Ten Steps to Setting Up a Streamlined Reality TV Show

- Ten Steps to Casting a Water-Cooler Reality TV Show

- Ten Steps to Producing a Signature Reality TV Show

- Ten Steps to Posting and Delivering an Airable Reality TV Show

- Ten Steps to Mastering the New Media Maze

www.movieinabox.com/books